# THE GUARANTEED TAX SAVINGS SYSTEM

# Robert Bennington

## Disclaimer Notice

While every attempt has been made to provide accurate information within this book, the author, publisher and the National Audit Defense Network will not accept responsibility for any claim, case study or legal situation mentioned herein. The author has discussed tax issues with former IRS agents and tax professionals for accuracy, but every reader is urged to consult a competent legal professional.

"Changes to the Internal Revenue Code are currently pending before the United States Congress. All information contained in this book is per the Internal Revenue Code and regulations in effect at press time. Readers should consult with competent legal counsel for the most current tax law information."

The author discussed stories of real people who have placed themselves in jeopardy with the IRS or other government officials and, while their stories need to be told, the author will not be responsible for any information to any person regarding the confidential material in the text. For security reasons, the author and National Audit Defense Network are unable to reveal any anonymous sources within the book or provide information for the same.

The National Audit Defense Network has not accepted nor will they accept any individual into the organization who has intentionally deceived the IRS, assuming they have informed NADN of such, and in no way condones or tolerates tax evasion or dishonesty.

Library of Congress Catalog Card Number: 2001116261

ISBN: 0-9708123-3-7


**Publisher:**
David Whitehead
The Printing Authority, Inc.
P.O. Box 458
Santa Clara, UT 84765
Telephone: (435) 986-0003

# Acknowledgments

I would like to express my gratitude to Cort Christie for his considerable time, contribution, and soundness of advice. Winner of the 1999 Ernst and Young *Entrepreneur of the Year Award*, Cort Christie has been active in the fiscal world throughout his life. He was the youngest financial consultant hired in his region by Merrill Lynch and Co. As Chief Executive Officer for National Audit Defense Network, Mr. Christie brings entrepreneurial, business and leadership skills to the NADN management team. His combined knowledge of business structuring, tax strategies, and leadership development processes, provide the expertise needed to spearhead the strategic evolvement of this fast growing company.

Mr. Christie conducts seminars around the country on entrepreneurial subjects including basic corporation fundamentals, advanced corporate strategies, asset protection and financial planning. He is known worldwide for his extensive knowledge of tax strategies and incorporating national enterprises that are experiencing rapid growth.

In addition to lecturing on corporate structuring, Mr. Christie is involved with educating the public about the sometimes hidden facets of the IRS and what it takes to avoid the dreaded tax audit. He has appeared on some of the largest radio shows across the country including Bo Gritz, Warren

Duffy, MSNBC and CNBC. Cort Christie also hosted his own radio show, *The Cort Christie Financial Program* which aired both in San Diego and Las Vegas.

Mr. Christie is also the CEO of Nevada Corporate Headquarters, Inc. (NCH), a business service firm based in Las Vegas, NV, credited with the formation of over 12,000 Nevada Corporations. NCH offers incorporation services, business development services, business financial services and educational seminars to its diverse client base consisting of thousands of companies from virtually every state in the nation.

Co-author of 1-800-AWAY IRS and author of Incorporating In Nevada , as well as numerous journal and newsletter articles about the IRS and tax strategy, Christie has a vast background and experience in financial businesses and marketing. He is a graduate from the University of Minnesota, Duluth, with a BA in Finance and expects to receive his MBA from Pepperdine University by 2003. Currently, Mr. Christie resides in Las Vegas with his wife, Jennifer, a recent law school graduate, and their two young children, Luke 9, and Lian 6.

# Table of Contents

# Chapter One

# Introduction

*"I wasted time, and now time doth waste me."*
**-William Shakespeare, *Richard III***

*"That government is best which governs least."*
**-Thomas Jefferson**

If you're like the average American citizen, last year somewhere close to half of your total income went to paying taxes. Another way of looking at this is that every penny you earned from January 1 until somewhere around the middle of May went to pay taxes of one form or another. This didn't just happen last year either. Almost six months out of each year you work is for the benefit of various taxing authority coffers.

Now what do they do with that money? Politicians like to say that they need the money to keep us safe from aggression and terrorism, build our roadways, maintain our national parks, educate our children, and research cures for cancer and other diseases. Needless to say, these are all fine objectives. The problem is that an alarmingly small percentage of the money you pay in taxes actually finds its way to highway workers and roadway construction, park rangers and trail maintenance, teachers and classrooms, and medical researchers and hospitals. Unfortunately, a large proportion of that money ends up in the pockets of politicians, administrators, and other bureaucrats who, from their limousines and over lavish lunches, pay themselves to decide where your tax dollars should go—and then oftentimes get it wrong anyway.

## What This Book Can Do For You

Thankfully, there are ways you can decrease the amount of money you payout for taxes. There are ways to structure your tax liability so that you don't end up spending half of what you earn on taxes. You won't have to wait until nearly June each calendar year to begin paying your own bills and maybe even pocketing some money for your retirement or your kids' college education.

This is exactly why I've written this book: to put tax strategies into simple and straightforward language which you can put into practice *legally* and thereby, in good conscience, reduce your tax liability. The word "legally" is very important here. Please make sure you read the section, "A Word To The Wise" at the end of this chapter.

I know that you work hard for your money, and I know that you'd like to spend it the way *you* want, not the way someone else wants you to spend it. I know that you've got better things to spend it on than some bloated bureaucrat's Jaguar or even on the top-heavy administrative costs of an otherwise worthwhile government program.

With that in mind, I've laid out in this book a number of specific ways you can dramatically reduce the amount of money you spend on taxes. I'll show you how you can turn a hobby into a home business. I'll introduce you to a variety of different types of corporations and show you the incredible tax-saving advantages of setting up a C Corporation. I'll show you how you can reduce the amount of estate and gift taxes you pay. Finally, I'll go over in detail the many ways you can increase the deductions you claim so that your taxable income is far less and your taxes far fewer.

One very important thing to keep in mind is that this book is intended to provide only the broadest of overviews. It will provide you with a range of your options—the possibilities available. In many cases, however, you will still need the assistance and/or consultation of a licensed tax specialist when initiating these suggestions. In some cases, you will need a financial-planning expert—if, for example, you want to set up a profit-sharing plan. As we will discuss later in this book, the tax law is so complex and ever-changing, that what works today will not necessarily work tomorrow. I do not say this to discourage you. The tax savings you will reap from pursuing the ideas you will find in this book well outweigh the time spent putting them into practice correctly as well as any money you may spend consulting with a tax professional.

This book is organized in such a way as to help you make the most of the information I have to offer. I begin with the most basic restructuring ideas and work through the book to more complex and advanced strategies. In addition, each chapter works the same way: I begin with some basic suggestions for those less familiar with the concepts; toward the end of the chapter, the ideas and suggestions are more complex and involved.

At the end of the book you will find a *glossary*, a list of definitions. These are words and phrases that are used throughout the book (as well as throughout the tax world) of which you should have a clear understanding. Keep in mind that these are very basic definitions and that the terms are defined more completely in other places in the book, where specificity and detail provide both context and consequence.

## A Word To The Wise

At the beginning of the last section, I mentioned that it is important that you use a trustworthy source when developing your tax strategies. There have been a growing number of so-called tax experts springing up lately making wild claims that often seem too good to be true.  Given the power of the government to come down heavily on tax evaders, it is extremely important that you know that the tax strategies you employ to reduce your tax liability come from a reputable source.

You may have heard or read one or more of the following claims:

"…Taxes are unconstitutional …" or "…the 16th Amendment was not properly ratified…" or "…wages do not constitute gross income…" or "…reporting and paying income taxes is strictly voluntary, so filing a tax return is not required…" and finally, "…the income tax is an 'excise' tax and an excise cannot be imposed on an individual… ."

Often these claims come from persuasive radio personalities, seemingly qualified seminar personalities, so-called "underground" newspapers and lately, via email.  Often the promoters of these arguments claim to have not filed tax returns or paid taxes for years (usually all of their income and assets are in their spouse's name, who does file taxes). These claims are well-written, well-spoken, and quote Supreme Court decisions, Congressional Records, State Court decisions and sometimes, sections of the Internal Revenue Code itself. The truth is, the promoters are taking bits of information out of the context in which they were written and twisting them into a new (self-serving) argument that, in the end, will NOT stand up in court. I say "self-serving" because oftentimes these promoters are attempting to sell the audience something, but will be long gone when the persons following their advice find themselves in deep water. Think about this: often, the very State Supreme Court decisions they are quoting are states that themselves permit an income tax.

## If it sounds too good to be true, it probably is!

The courts are so tired of hearing these arguments that, in fact, they have deemed them "frivolous" and are assessing the government's legal fees against the taxpayers filing these claims in court. In addition, the courts are upholding the IRS's imposition of a special "frivolous return penalty". Consequently, individuals who follow the advice of these promoters are not only finding themselves with a whopping bill for back taxes, interest and penalties, but also for the special frivolous return penalty AND if taken all the way to court, the IRS's legal fees as well.

I know it is very tempting to want to follow a few very vocal individuals who say they have been getting away with not paying any taxes for years. As stated above, what they often do (but fail to tell you), is put all assets and income in their spouse's name. So although they *personally* may not pay any taxes, their family unit does. Remember: "If it sounds too good to be true, it probably is!"

The strategies you will read about in this book have been developed by the tax professionals at National Audit Defense Network (NADN). NADN is a network of former IRS agents, CPAs, Tax Attorneys and Enrolled Agents who have switched sides and now work on behalf of the American taxpayer. Collectively, they have hundreds of years of knowledge and expertise which you, the average taxpayer, can now put to use.

You *CAN* trust that these strategies not only work, but also that they are indeed legal. However, I don't believe you should just take my word for it so before we get into the actual strategies, we're going to take a look at this tax code that everyone talks about, as well as the history of taxes, and how we got to where we are today.

# Chapter Two

# Taxes: Nothing New

*"And it came to pass in those days, that there went out a decree from Caesar Augustus, that all the world should be taxed."*
**-The Bible, Luke: 2:1**

*'It was as true,' said Mr. Barkis, 'as taxes is. And nothing's truer than them.'"*
**-Charles Dickens, *David Copperfield***

Though certain kinds of specific taxes are relatively new to human societies, taxation itself is nearly as old as the human race. It has certainly been around as long as man has needed to govern himself. In days long gone, of course, there was no such thing as separation of church and state; the church was state, and vice versa. Usually, those in charge were what we might today call ministers or priests, holy men of some kind. Often elevated to positions somewhere between their lowly human subjects and the gods themselves, this ministerial class often took its sustenance in the form of "gifts" such as grain, cattle, wine, or even tea, as was the case in ancient China.

By the time the Romans ruled the vast majority of civilization, taxation had taken the form of a type of "protectionism." Citizens of conquered lands were forced to pay one way or another (sometimes in several ways), for the benefits of being part of the

Roman republic. In addition to having to pay in coin, they often had to pay with military service. Roman citizens, on the other hand, were generally exempt from such "taxes."

Many historians, in fact, claim that the decline of the Roman Empire was directly related to its system of taxation. While revenue generated from conquered outlying areas flowed into Rome proper, the money was used both to finance the military and for what we might today call "social programs," including the policy of free grain for all Roman citizens. Eventually however, Rome began to run out of lands to conquer and foreigners to tax, and inevitably had to impose taxes on its citizens as well to pay for that military and free grain. Ultimately, the argument goes, Rome was internally corrupted, its economy ruined by excessive taxation. By the time the barbarians were climbing over the walls, the city was in no shape to defend itself.

One early form of tax collecting was "tax farming." Under this method, a citizen was licensed by the state to collect taxes, upon which he was paid a percentage or commission. The rest he turned over to the government.

During the Middle Ages, taxation often took the form of tolls and customs fees from merchants. This was a real advantage to localities, as the burden generally fell on passersby rather than on residents. If a shoemaker were passing through town with a wagonload of merchandise, he would perhaps be taxed a percentage of the weight of his load. During the 13th century, England's Parliament imposed "tonnage and poundage" fees on wine, wool, and leather in order to extract money from traveling Italian merchants. As you can imagine, this unfair encumbrance didn't generally go over well. In fact, Charles I of England was sent to the guillotine, in part, because he stuck his neck out too far in taxing his subjects.

Later in the Middle Ages, tax collecting got more sophisticated as royalty targeted  more and more people to bankroll their excesses. King Henry VIII may be best known for such things as beheading wives who wouldn't bear him sons and for creating new religions out of thin air when existing ones didn't meets his needs. However, he was also a master at taxation strategy.   In his employ was one John Morton, who devised what came to be known as "Morton's Fork." All it took was keeping a careful eye on their subjects' spending.  If one of the king's noblemen didn't seem to be spending very much, then it was assumed he had plenty of money stashed away that could be taken for use by the crown. If, on the other hand, he was spending extravagantly, then it was assumed that he had plenty to share, and it too would be taken for use by the crown. Etymologists might dispute me here, but this could very well be the origin such phrases as "fork it over," and getting "forked" by the government.

The founding of the United States of America was, as every school child knows, in part a reaction against much of what merry ol' England stood for and had attempted to bring to the New World. Though ultimately the American Revolution was very much a reaction to over-taxation as well as, of course, "taxation without representation," early colonists lived more or less free from government interference.  For example, exports from the colonies were originally subject to the Acts of Trade and Navigation which dictated that shipments from the New World had to go through England.  Upon arriving, taxes were levied on these exports before being sent on to the rest of Europe. However, because those tariffs (oftentimes ridiculously steep) were levied after they arrived in

England and passed on to customers, the American exporters were for the most part not subject to these taxes. Even when taxes were levied on the American colonies, they were quite easy to avoid. This was partly because the crown, based on the other side of the Atlantic, had trouble collecting from such a distance. Several attempts were made to unify the colonies under an umbrella that would have the authority to tax, yet because the colonies were so fiercely independent, these plans never bore fruit.

Eventually the English found themselves defending their newly established colonies. The French and Indian Wars, Pontiac's Rebellion, and other military exercises cost the British dearly, and the government needed a way to pay those expenses. Guess who got the bill? That's right, the colonies.

Beginning in the mid-1760s, King George III began to levy taxes on the colonists, beginning with 1764's Revenue Act, which taxed sugar, molasses, silk, and wine. The next step was the Stamp Act of 1765, which taxed printed matter, ranging from playing cards to legal documents, and had to be paid in British sterling rather than colonial currency. This infuriated the colonists, who responded by abusing and harassing their British governors and establishing the Stamp Act Congress, representatives of nine colonies who met in New York City to deal with the problem. Britain in turn responded with Parliament's declaring it legal to tax the colonies and at the same time tossing the colonists a bone by repealing the Stamp Act.

In 1767, the British government passed the Townshend Acts, which taxed trade, tightened anti-smuggling laws, and provided for better collection of duties. Needless to say, these acts were not tolerated well by the colonists either. In retaliation, the colonists instigated a "non-importation movement, " a boycott of all taxed goods. The Townshend Acts, too, were repealed, in 1770, although they kept in place the tax on tea, largely as a symbolic attempt of an in-your-face show of British superiority. Of course, we all know this action led to the famous Boston Tea Party. Similar actions to the infamous tea party also took place in the middle and southern colonies. These acts finally led the British to take military action. Thus was born the American Revolution.

# Chapter Three

# From The Boston Tea Party to a 6,000 Page Tax Code: How Did We Get Here?

*" 'I fear those big words,' Stephen said, 'which make us so unhappy.' "*
**-James Joyce, *Ulysses***

*"Our life is frittered away by detail ...simplify, simplify."*
**-Henry David Thoreau, *Walden***

Some of the most basic principles on which the United States of America was founded are, in fact, contradictory in nature. Because of this, there have been struggles from the beginning—especially in areas such as taxation. While the framers of the U.S. Constitution sought to unify the states under one central government, they also sought to give each state "sovereignty, freedom, and independence," so as to keep that newly-formed central government from becoming too powerful. In an attempt to keep that balance healthy, the framers designed a three-part series of economic pillars, as outlined in Article I of the Constitution:

No state shall, without the consent of Congress, lay any imports or duties on imports or exports.

The Congress shall have the power to lay and collect taxes, duties, imports, and excises to pay its debts and provide for the common defense and general welfare of the United States, but all duties, imports, and excises, shall be uniform throughout the United States.

No capitation or other direct tax shall be levied unless it is in proportion to the census.

It can be concluded from the above that: states would not be permitted to tax trade; Congress had to treat all states equally and; the amount of tax the government could levy had to be directly related to the number of people the government was serving.

At the same time, Article VIII of the Articles of Confederation states:

All charges of war, and all other expenses that shall be incurred for the common defense or general welfare, and allowed by the United States in Congress assembled, shall be defrayed out of a common treasury, which shall be supplied by the several States in proportion to the value of all land within each State...The taxes for paying that proportion shall be laid and levied by the authority and direction of the legislatures of the several States within the time agreed upon by the United States in Congress assembled.

These statements have led to over two centuries of debate by politicians, attorneys, tax experts, pundits, and writers in "Letters to the Editor" columns across the country. For example, what exactly is meant by "direct tax" in Article I of the Constitution? Does that include income tax? Apparently, even during the debates at the Constitutional Convention the question of income tax went unanswered, although for the first 80 years or so of the republic, "direct taxes" took on the definition of taxes on land and capitation taxes.

Things changed, however. The first United States income taxes were "emergency" taxes, imposed to finance specific projects, usually wars. President Lincoln enacted such a tax during the Civil War (one which included inheritance taxes as well) but it was repealed in 1870. The next half century would see the courts continually reinterpreting the constitution and, as the government's need for money began to take a larger role in controlling policy, the federal government was granted more and more power to levy taxes.

## A Look at the United States Tax Code

In the case of any such trade or business in which the income is computed under an accrual method, the gross income from such trade or business, adjusted in accordance with the provisions of paragraphs (1) through (7) and paragraph (9) of this subsection; and, for the purposes of such sentence, if an individual (including a member of a partnership) derives gross income from more than one such trade or business, such gross income (including his distributive share of the gross income of any partnership derived from any such trade or business) shall be deemed to have been derived from one trade or business.

The preceding sentence and clauses (i) through (iv) of the second preceding sentence shall also apply in the case of nay trade or business (other than a trade or business specified in such second preceding sentence) which is carried on by an individual who is self-employed on a regular basis as defined in subsection (h), or by a partnership of which an individual is a member on a regular basis as defined in subsection 9h), buy only if such individual's net earnings from self-employment as determined without regard to this sentence in the taxable year are less than $1,600 and less than 662/3 percent of the sum (in such taxable year) of such individual's gross income derived from all trades or businesses carried on by him and his distributive share of the income or loss from all trades or businesses carried on by all the partnerships of which he is a member; except that this sentence shall not apply to more than 5 taxable years in the case of any individual, and in no case in which an individual elects to determine the amount of his net earnings from self-employment for a taxable year under the provisions of the two preceding sentences with respect to a trade or business to which the second preceding sentence applies and with respect to a trade or business to which this sentence applies shall such net earnings for such years exceed $1,600.

United States Tax Code, Section 1402(a)(vi)

# A Tax Code With 6000 Pages of Text

I don't know about you, but when I was in eighth grade English, my teacher said never, ever write a run-on sentence because anyone reading it would lose track of what was at the beginning by the time they reached the end. Now either the writers of the U.S. Tax Code didn't have an English teacher as good as mine, or they want average taxpayers like us to give up even trying to read (let alone understand) it. Like Section 1402 above, the entire tax code is one long series of run-on sentences, making it extremely difficult to follow. One could argue that it only makes sense that the United States Tax Codes would grow more complicated and complex over the years. And grow more complicated it has. The 1955 Tax Code ran about 750,000 words; as we begin the new millennium, the code is running at over six million words. Former presidential candidate, U.S. senator, and pro basketball player Bill Bradley called our tax system "overly complex"—and that was back in the mid-1980s. In fact, if the current United States Tax Code were to be printed out on letter-size paper, with sixty lines per page, the document would run 6,000 pages.

As Thoreau penned in Walden, "Our life is frittered away by detail…simplify, simplify." Of course things are somewhat different today from how they were in Thoreau's time. It's doubtful that anyone could actually work only six weeks a year and earn enough money to live as Thoreau did in the mid-19th century. Some things are not all that different, however. When Thoreau refused to pay taxes that were used in supporting the Mexican-American War to which he was morally opposed, he was sentenced to jail time.

# Solutions to Simplify the Tax Code

Naturally, there have been attempts to simplify the system, including an ongoing call for a "flat tax," by which everyone—everyone—would be required to pay taxes at the same rate. Flat-tax proponents usually suggest a figure somewhere around 13% as a number sufficient to support current government programs. They claim that the savings from simplifying the form alone would be immense, and that all the information the IRS needs could fit on a form the size of a postcard.

Proponents of a national sales tax comprise another group of tax reformers. They too postulate this as the fairest and simplest way to tax the populace. However, until such time as a new taxing system is put into place, we can only look to Congress and the Administrative Branch to institute changes which may or may not simplify the tax code—usually they do not simplify the tax code.

One of President Ronald Reagan's important acts, about halfway through his second term, was signing into law the *Tax Reform Act of 1986*. This massive rewrite of the tax code did away with many of the tax loopholes that had existed up until that point. Even so, it seems that wasn't enough. There was also a *Revenue Act of 1987* and the *Technical and Miscellaneous Revenue Act of 1988*.

In fact, while the *Internal Revenue Service Restructuring and Reform Act of 1998* sought to reverse the trend toward incomprehensibility, the act really made the code even more complicated by adding thousands of new pages of law. In 2001, Congress passed the Bush Administration's Economic Growth and Tax relief Reconciliation Act (EGTRA). While EGTRA slashed tax rates across the board, it did little to simplify the tax code.

# The Tax Code Goes to Court

The United State Tax Code is not the sole source for defining the country's tax structure. Not only is it important to have at least a basic understanding of the Tax Code in order to avoid being taken advantage of by the government, but today's taxpayer also needs to realize that the code is constantly being interpreted and reinterpreted by the country's judiciary system. Cases are continually being heard, decided, appealed, and overturned by the United State Tax Court, the United States District Court, and the United States Claims Court. What might have been a legitimate tax deduction in 1999, for example, might not be next year. In discussions about the United States system of taxation, indeed the term "case by case" is most appropriate.

Consider this classic example:  In 1984, the United States Court of Appeals for the Second Circuit [Weissman v. Commissioner (751 F2d 512)] overturned a case that had ruled that a professor at City College of New York could not claim a home office deduction. The professor asserted that in order to maintain his teaching position he was forced to work between 64 and 75 hours a week, yet the college administration did not provide adequate resources so that he could safely and effectively work there. Thus, he spent at least 80% of those hours at home. The court found that he could legally claim a home office deduction within the parameters of the United States Tax Code.

Of course, scores of cases have been heard since then, and the Tax Code has been revised over a dozen times. In fact, the definition of "home office" was dramatically changed in 1999—those changes will be discussed later in the book—as were hundreds of other important definitions and interpretations.

If Henry David Thoreau were alive today, he'd be absolutely

appalled. "Simplify, simplify," he would say.

# Chapter Four

# Taxes in the 20th Century

*"Well, fancy giving money to the government!*
*Might as well have put it down the drain.*
*Fancy giving money to the government!*
*Nobody will see the stuff again."*
**-A.P. Herbert, *Too Much!***

*"The hardest thing in the world to*
*understand is income tax."*
**-Albert Einstein**

As stated in the last chapter, the government's need for money began to take a larger role in controlling policy throughout the 19th century. The debate over what was meant by a "direct tax" was continuous. While it may seem obvious to us that an income tax would be a "direct tax," it is not clear that is what the Founding Fathers meant by the term. During the debates at the Constitutional Convention, a delegate asked what "direct taxes" meant, but received no answer.

By the end of the Civil War, it seemed that the term "direct taxes" had come to mean only capitation taxes and taxes on land. However, much resistance to a tax on income continued to exist throughout the country, and in 1895, the U.S. Supreme Court stepped in to give some input on their interpretation of what could and could not be taxed. It was clear that some measure needed to be taken to resolve the issue. The response from Congress was the 16th Amendment to the Constitution.

## The 16th Amendment Opens the Gateway

The Congress shall have power to lay and collect taxes on incomes, from whatever source derived, without apportionment among the several states, and without regard to any census of enumeration.

-16th Amendment to the Constitution, 1913

In 1895 the U.S. Supreme Court's decision held that the income tax act was unconstitutional; specifically it stated that income tax on real property was not allowed as a direct tax (Pollock vs. Farmer's Loan and Trust Company). At that time, however, income tax on professions, wages, trades, or vocations was held to be constitutionally valid. So that there would be no question in the future, the country ratified the 16th Amendment to the Constitution to specifically overrule Pollock. Whether this was done by inventive definitions and re-definitions of the term "direct tax" or by resorting to the pre-Pollock history of the excise tax, the government had recovered most of its power to tax incomes. The 16th Amendment allowed Congress to lay and collect taxes on income from whatever source derived; it also allowed passage of the *Income Tax Act of 1913,* the predecessor to the current Internal Revenue Code. Since that time, there have been numerous attempts to get the courts to hold that the Income Tax Code is unconstitutional. One of the arguments has been that the 16th Amendment was ratified incorrectly. However, the U.S. Supreme Court has ruled that the 16th Amendment was ratified properly; thus the government can pretty much tax whatever it chooses.

Many tax reformers and tax experts trace the beginnings of excessive tax on Americans directly to the 16th Amendment, ratified shortly after Woodrow Wilson's election to the presidency. Among Wilson's early acts, he signed laws reducing U.S. tariffs and then compensated for lost revenue by imposing progressive taxes on Americans—both on individuals and corporations. Exemptions, however, were relatively high. All individuals with less than $3,000 and married couples with less than $4,000 were exempted from paying the income tax. This effectively removed 98% of the population from the tax rolls. Tax rates began at 1% with a ceiling set at 7%.

World War I was a costly endeavor for the United States and it needed to be financed. To that end, deductions were reduced by roughly 50% increasing substantially the number of Americans on the tax rolls to approximately 15%. Additionally, the rates themselves were raised dramatically, topping out at 77% for individuals and 64% for corporations. After the war, rates were lowered although when the Depression hit, poverty rates rose sky-high, and the government sought ways to reduce it.

# The Beginning of Social Security

In 1935, the new Social Security program was one response specifically targeted to the increasing poverty rates among the elderly (50% in the mid 1930s). The idea behind the new Social Security program was to provide old age, survivor, and disability benefits to every eligible American citizen. It was designed so current workers would support current retirees, on the promise that they, in turn, would be supported in their retirement. The idea was that a relatively small part of each worker's income, as a payroll tax, would be deposited in an interest-earning fund from which that worker would ultimately be able to draw.

During the 1940's came World War II and the huge costs associated with such a massive endeavor: supporting American troops, building aircraft, transporting equipment and machinery, etc. Ultimately, this led the U.S. to re-examine its tax base, resulting, naturally, in an increase of amounts that American individuals and corporations contributed to the federal government. They in turn would decide in what manner those moneys would be spent. At the height of World War II, as many as 90% of American workers were contributing, in the form of income tax, to the government's coffers— those making $200,000 or more paid as much as 94% of their income in taxes. From that period on, income tax simply became a fact of American life.

## World War II until Today

Save for a brief rise to finance the Korean War, taxes remained fairly stable between the end of World War II and 1962. Individual exemptions were set at $600, while the tax rate topped out at 91% on income over $400,000. Then in 1963, Congress enacted a series of tax cuts, financed by inflation and a tax code that was not indexed. This ultimately led to artificially inflated individual incomes which pushed taxpayers into higher tax brackets. It was also during this time, and in the years between the Kennedy and Reagan presidencies, that the tax code grew more and more complex and that the Internal Revenue Service began to assume powers that gave pause to, and frightened, many, many Americans.

When Ronald Reagan was elected in 1980, one of his first acts was to effectively index the tax brackets and the personal exemption. Ultimately, Reagan lowered marginal rates resulting in the short-term effect of decreased revenue, but the long-term effect of stimulated economic activity. This increased revenue by about $90 billion per year over the eight years of his presidency.

As federal spending outpaced federal income, however, the budget deficit grew to horrendous figures. Attempts to slow the out-of-control deficit led to several measures, including *Gramm-Rudman-Hollings Act* and the George Bush-Dick Darman Budget Deal, which contributed to Bush's defeat in the election of 1992.

With Bill Clinton's election came a number of tax increases, including what Senator Pat Moynihan (D-New York), called the "largest increase in history." Curiously, as the 1990s wound down and we began the new millennium, the United States' economy was healthier than it had been in generations. Whether this was due to Clinton's maneuverings, to the Republican-controlled House and Senate, or to Federal Reserve Board Chairman Alan Greenspan, could be debated for years. In all likelihood, however, the burgeoning economy was at least partly the result of a technology that did more to change the way we view the world than any other development in the course of human events. Perhaps politicians were only flattering themselves by thinking they had anything to do with it.

The passage of EGTRA in 2001 produced another sweeping change in tax law. Written to promote economic growth by lowering the effective tax rate all Americans pay, the Act also made sweeping changes to retirement plans and began the phase-out of the Death Tax.

Though people continue to debate, among other things, the value of taxes, how best to collect tax, which programs should be funded, etc., almost everyone agrees on one thing: the American system of taxation needs reform. In fact, almost everyone would agree on two parts of that reform: first, the tax code needs to be simplified; and second, the Internal Revenue Service must be both less powerful and more accountable. Whether that will happen remains to be seen as changes are a long time in the making.

## Possibilities for Simplification

As stated earlier, many have proposed a simplified tax system they believe would do away with the inequities of our current system. One of these proposals is a "flat tax," by which everyone would be taxed at the same rate, say 13%. Our system today, however, is known as a "progressive tax" system. This system is based on the philosophy that the rich should contribute more to make the government work than the poor; in other words, the more money you make, the more you pay. As you move into higher income brackets, that income is taxed at a higher rate. Imagine each time you increase your income by $1000, you increase your tax rate by 10%:

| Amount Earned | % Taxed | Amount Paid | % of Income Taxed |
|---|---|---|---|
| $1,000 | 10% | $100 | 10% |
| $2,000 | 10% on first $1,000; 20% on second $1,000 | $300 | 15% |
| $3,000 | 10% on first $1,000; 20% on second $1,000; 30% on third $1,000 | $600 | 20% |

Now, that seems pretty straightforward, right? The problem is, the United State Tax Code has taken that concept and complicated it to the point that it's 6,000 pages long. Of course, there need to be explanations, qualifications, considerations, exceptions, and so on. The code is now so complex, it's virtually incomprehensible. Additionally, the Internal Revenue Service produces hundreds of different forms to use in filing your taxes. That means that most of us need help. We hire CPAs and other tax professionals to helps us through the quagmire although oftentimes they're simply filling in blanks themselves and not working from the tax code per se. It also means that the more you can afford to pay, the better your chances of finding loopholes and other ways to decrease the amount you pay. This is not simply because you can afford expensive tax-preparation services, but also because some of the loopholes are intentionally designed for higher income taxpayers. Meanwhile the low-end wage earner, who has neither the ability to pay for tax preparation nor the education to know he should, ends up paying more. Most agree that the Internal Revenue Service itself has grown too big for its britches. As an arm of the government, the IRS should simply, and literally be the citizens, "we the people." No matter how conservative we might be when it comes to paying our taxes, we all seem to want to give the IRS as wide a berth as possible. After all, we've all heard the stories: bullying IRS agents and auditors, assets being seized, wealthy celebrities being reduced to paupers after IRS raids. Most people prefer to keep a low profile.  Unfortunately, in part because of the complicated demands made on taxpayers, and the fact that it wields such power, most workers are either afraid of or angry with the IRS—or both.

# NADN's Philosophy

Fear and anger should not control how we view a branch of our government, which, theoretically anyway, we have put in place to serve us, something needs to be done.  We at the National Audit Defense Network continue to lobby for changes in the American taxation system.  Even though we might appear skeptical, even cynical, at times (an attitude resulting from direct contact with the IRS and taxpayers who call us daily with IRS horror stories), we maintain hope that at least some of the mess can be cleaned up.  In the meantime, however, it is our philosophy that each and every taxpayer should use the current tax code to their benefit.  It is to that end, this book has been written.

# Chapter Five

# Making the System Work For You

*"We can inform Jonathan what are inevitable consequences of being too fond of glory; —Taxes upon every article which enters the mouth, or covers the back, or is placed under foot...taxes on everything on earth, and the waters under the earth."*
**-Rev. Sydney Smith,**
**Review of Seybert's *Statistical Annals of the United States***

*"As a citizen, you...have an obligation to yourself to know your rights under the law and possible tax deductions. And to claim every one of them."*
**-Donald Alexander,**
**former IRS Commissioner under 3 Presidents**

To itemize or not to itemize. If you've ever pondered this, let me state right now, the best way to realize tax savings is to itemize. You may think it is not worth the trouble, however, once you begin putting your records in order (and with the helpful tips from this book) you will be amazed at the number of deductions and credits you will be able to take. The key is in planning.

Don't wait until January (or worse, April) to begin pulling together your tax information from the previous year. Come January you should be starting your tax planning for the upcoming year. If you're reading this in preparation for filing your last year's tax returns, go ahead and set up files for this year while you're sorting your records and receipts for last year. Remember, the bulk of the work is in getting started and getting organized. Once you do that, you'll only have to spend 10 seconds a day putting your receipts in a safe place.

## Checklist of Records and Receipts

Before you start to prepare your return, collect all the records, statements, and receipts you have that are listed in the following checklist. You may need these types of records for preparing your return. You will also want to sort out your checks, credit card statements, bills and receipts by category (i.e. medical expenses, travel and entertainment, mileage logs, charitable donations, etc.)

- **W-2 forms.** You should receive at least three copies: one for your federal tax return, one for your state tax return, and one for your records. The easiest way to keep track of your Form W–2 copy is to staple it to the copy of your tax return that you keep, just as you staple a copy of the Form W-2 to the copy of your tax return that you send to the IRS.
- **1099 forms.** Unless your Form 1099 includes tax withholding, do not file it with your tax return. Save it for your records. If your Form 1099 shows federal tax withheld, attach a copy to your tax return to receive credit for the withholding.
- **Schedule K-1 forms.** Keep the forms that you receive

from partnerships, S corporations, estates, and trusts; do not attach them to your tax return.

• **Year-end statements.** Save the statements that report the interest you earned from bank accounts.

• **Year-end brokerage statements.** These statements indicate purchases and sales of securities, dates and amounts of such transactions, margin interest, broker fees, the history of reinvested dividends, and interest and dividends earned during the year (including tax-exempt interest and dividends.)

• **Financial statements.** Financial statements summarize your income and expenses from a business that you operate, a farm, or rental property that you own.

• **Receipts.** Save receipts for prescription drugs you purchased during the year, canceled checks or credit card statements, and accompanying bills for medical expenses paid during the year. If you are self-employed, save canceled checks and bills for health insurance.

• **Property tax statements for your house.** If you pay your property tax through your mortgage company, the mortgage company summarizes this amount on your annual mortgage report.

Vehicle registration summary. Keep this if you live in a state that attaches an excise tax to the purchase of license plates.

• **Mortgage interest statement Form 1098.** This statement summarizes the mortgage interest you paid during the year and any real estate tax paid on your behalf by your mortgage company.

• **Closing statements.** If you bought or sold a home or other real property during the year, you may need information from the closing statements, such as interest and property tax adjustments.

• **Record of charitable donations.** For cash donations, keep your canceled checks as well as the receipt you got from the agency or person that received the donations. The receipt should indicate how much of your payment is tax deductible and what, if anything, you got in return for your contribution. For donations of noncash items, keep a detailed list of what you donated, when you made the donation, to whom you made the donation, your estimated value of the goods you donated, and how you arrived at that value. Be sure to keep a receipt from the person or agency that received the donations showing that you did not receive anything in return for your contribution.

• **Records of business expenses.** Save automobile logs and receipts for business travel, meals, and entertaining—including details such as the names of those you entertained or bought meals for, when and where the meals or entertainment were purchased, and the nature of the business that was discussed or performed. A calendar can be a convenient place for tracking this information about your business expenses.

By assessing your financial situation for the year at the beginning of the year, you can be proactive in your decision making instead of reactive. For example, if you're buying tax shelters, the earlier in the year you go into them, the better, as many deductions for tax shelters are dependent on the amount of time spent in the venture. Another area in which early planning is essential is the buying and selling of stock.

# Trading In Securities

A trader in securities is a person who buys and sells securities in frequent and continuous operations for their own account rather than for the account of customers. A dealer in securities deals with the accounts of customers. To qualify as a "trader" you must be regularly engaged in such activities to the extent that it would qualify as a trade or business. You must be actively and continuously occupied in the purchase and sale of securities with your time and energy devoted to such work at least part-time. Pursuit of short-term trades as opposed to long-term capital gain is characteristic of a trader.

If you meet the above tests, you may deduct your expenses from gross income on a Schedule C in determining adjusted gross income. The advantages here are that these business expenses are not subject to the 2% AGI limitation on miscellaneous itemized deductions nor are they tax preference items for purposes of the alternative minimum tax as they would be if they were miscellaneous itemized deductions. Commissions on the purchase of securities must increase the purchase price, and are not deductible as business expenses currently for a trader. Commissions on sales are deductible business expenses to a dealer in securities, but not to a trader or an investor.

Finally, a trader in securities, unlike a dealer, reports the income from sales on Schedule D which means you would not be subject to the self-employment tax on the income from the sale of securities (i.e., stocks, bonds, etc.). However, remember that the trader's business expenses are reported on Schedule C.

## Making the Most of Your Stock Losses

At the time of this writing, we are experiencing a very volatile stock market. When the value of your stock goes down, you get that sinking feeling—you've lost money. But the tax law doesn't allow that loss until you sell the stock. In a way that's good, because it means you can control the timing of your deduction, taking it when the benefit is the greatest.

The problem is, you may have a conflict. You want to deduct the loss, but you also want to keep the stock because you think it's going to bounce back. It's tempting to think you can sell the stock and claim the loss, then buy it back right away. And that's where the "wash sale" rule comes into play. If you buy replacement stock shortly after the sale—or shortly before the sale—you cannot deduct your loss. The government calls this a "wash sale."

In general, you have a wash sale if you sell stock at a loss, and buy substantially identical securities within 30 days before or after the sale. Example: On March 31 you sell 100 shares of XYZ at a loss. On April 10 you buy 100 shares of XYZ. The sale on March 31 is a wash sale. The wash sale period for any sale at a loss consists of 61 days: the day of the sale, the 30 days before the sale and the 30 days after the sale. *Note:* these are calendar days, not trading days. Count carefully! If you want to claim your loss as a deduction, you need to avoid purchasing the same stock during the wash sale period. For a sale on March 31, the wash sale period includes all of March and April.

The wash sale rule can apply even if you don't acquire stock. If you enter into a contract or option to acquire stock, that's enough to make the wash sale rule apply. Your sale of stock can also be a wash sale if, within the wash sale period, you sell a put option on the same stock that's "deep in the money." And you can have a wash sale from selling options at a loss, too. The wash sale rule actually has three consequences:

1. You are NOT allowed to claim the loss on your sale.
2. Your disallowed loss is added to the basis of the replacement stock.
3. Your holding period for the replacement stock includes the holding period of the stock you sold.

The basis adjustment is important because it preserves the benefit of the disallowed loss. You'll receive that benefit on a future sale of the replacement stock. You can see how what you sell and when you sell it can have a dramatic impact on your tax consequences. The holding period is also important. When you make a wash sale, your holding period for the replacement stock includes the period you held the stock you sold that generated the disallowed loss. This rule prevents you from converting what was a long-term loss into a short-term loss.

## Investing in Real Estate

Ownership of real estate has always been a wealth-building method of choice for many Americans at all levels of the economic pyramid. It is said of the late billionaire Howard Hughes that he never sold a piece of real estate; he only continued to buy it when possible. Today in Las Vegas, many of the acres that Hughes purchased for low prices in the 1970s are being developed and sold for very large profits in the affluent Summerlin development district. In Marina del Rey in Los Angeles, lands Hughes bought in the 1940s for his Hughes Aircraft Co. have been developed into expensive subdivisions.

"But," you say, "I don't have the money of a Howard Hughes!" Well, in order to make money and save taxes, you don't need Hughes' type money.   Besides, Howard didn't save much on taxes by buying raw land, even though he realized fantastic capital gains.

The secrets of making real estate work for you to save on taxes can be summarized in two words—Depreciation and Leverage. I will describe for you a typical scenario you might work out to make these secrets work for you.   In the following outline, I make some reasonable assumptions about certain facts that may not exactly fit your situation. However, by changing them slightly to conform to your local real estate market conditions, you will find that the general principles are sound and will work for you.

First, you need some capital to invest. "Oh, I thought there was a catch somewhere!" I hear you say. Well, if you don't have the capital required, borrow it. The interest you pay on money borrowed to invest can be deducted as an expense attributable to the rental property.

With your newly acquired capital (or your savings capital), use $10,314 as a down payment on a rental house, duplex or apartment building as large as you can purchase in your home market. Don't go too far from home to find your investment property since you want to keep close oversight on it, at least in the early years. You should be able to find a good property available with a 10% down payment.   So now you own a rental property with a market value of $103,140. That's where the leverage comes in. With 10% down, you are controlling property of 10 times the value of your investment.

Since you want to bring in the factor of depreciation to realize your tax savings, you next have to calculate how much depreciation you can claim on this new property. Land is not subject to depreciation, so you first subtract the land value. A reasonable ratio of land value to total value is 20%, so subtract 20% from your property value, leaving $82,508 available to depreciate.

Residential real estate is required by tax law to be depreciated at a constant value (so-called "straight-line depreciation") over 27 1/2 years. Your first year will be a partial year depending on the month in which you make your acquisition. After that, the rate per year is 3.636%, which calculates out to a value of $3000 depreciation deduction.

By purchasing this property at 10% down, you will probably have little or no "cash flow," meaning money in your pocket after paying expenses and mortgage payments out of the rental income, and, if you balance income and expenses properly, you also will have no cash expense out of pocket. But, you will have the $3000 depreciation deduction, which means you have a $3000 tax loss for the year. You use this loss to offset $3000 of other income you have and, if you are in the 28% tax bracket, you have saved $840 in taxes.

But why stop here? Just invest more money, get more losses and wipe out your entire tax bill! Well, not so fast; that is a good idea, but only a maximum of  $25,000 in passive losses may be used as an offset against income tax. In addition, once your income exceeds $100,000, the amount of these losses is reduced. However, the losses are not lost. You just have to carry them forward to some year when you meet the requirements for using them.

Your tax savings of $840 amounts to a return on investment of 8.1% on your investment of $10,314—better than a savings account but not as good as the stock market (if you're lucky). But don't forget that while you are saving all those taxes, the Howard Hughes factor is at work and your property is appreciating in value if it is typical of most real estate in the US. (There are areas where real estate has gone down in value, but naturally you aren't going to pick one of those.)

Now, you have followed our advice, bought an apartment building, saved on taxes for several years and your property has a substantial increase in value. What to do now? Sell and take your profits? No, because you would have to pay taxes on the increase in value, which even at the lower capital gain rates would take a big bite out of your earnings. Instead, you should make a tax-deferred exchange of your property into a larger one, and put off paying taxes to the "never-never," or whenever you ultimately sell your holdings.

## Becoming a Statutory Employee

Another tax strategy becoming more and more popular is becoming a "statutory employee." As a statutory employee, you would receive special treatment for deducting un-reimbursed business expenses. Statutory employees who qualify under Internal Revenue Code § 3121(d)(3) can use Schedule C to deduct their expenses instead of Schedule A [Rev. Rul. 90-93]. *Advantage:* Business expenses are NOT subject to the 2% AGI limitation on miscellaneous itemized deductions. In addition, business expenses are not a tax preference item for purposes of the alternative minimum tax as they would be if they were miscellaneous itemized deductions. *Note:* whenever possible, classify deductions so that they do not fall into the "miscellaneous itemized deductions" category.

The term "statutory employees" includes:

1. A full-time traveling or city salesperson. The salesperson must be one who solicits orders from wholesalers, restaurants, or similar establishments, on behalf of a principal. The merchandise sold must be for resale (i.e., food sold to a restaurant) or for supplies used in the buyer's business.

2. A full-time life insurance sales agent whose principal business activity is selling life insurance and/or annuity contracts for one life insurance company.

3. An agent-driver or commission-driver engaged in distributing meat, vegetables, bakery goods, beverages (other than milk), or laundry or dry cleaning services.

4. A home worker performing work on materials or goods furnished by the employer.

Of course, there is an even better way to increase your income AND realize significant tax savings...better than all the ideas mentioned above.

## Starting a Home-Based Business

One of the best strategies of which you can take advantage as an individual taxpayer is starting a home-based business for yourself. There are tremendous advantages to operating a business out of your home. Of course, the biggest advantage to running your own business is the opportunity for you to make some money, or to supplement your existing income. What could be better than to make a little extra money by getting paid for what you do anyway? Additionally, operating your own business offers a sense of pride and independence that working for someone else often doesn't.

I want to discuss the tax advantages of operating your own home business. First, you're going to be able to take everyday expenses, as they relate to that business, and write them off. In some cases, this means picking up an extra 30-40% in purchasing power by reducing your overall tax liability and thereby decreasing the amount of taxes you pay each year to the Internal Revenue Service.

What kind of business can you run out of your home that the IRS will recognize as legitimate? And just what kinds of losses and expenses are you allowed to write off? Well, in truth, you can run just about any kind of business, and as long as the loss or expense is related to it, you can write some or all of it off. You could babysit your neighbors' children, and write off the cost of the Dr. Seuss books you buy to entertain them. You could fix motorcycles in your garage and write off your tools. You could offer oboe lessons and write off the electricity you use to heat and light your studio. You could edit newsletters and write off your computer and software. You could build doghouses and write off a subscription to Dog Fancier Magazine. You could repair video equipment and write off the cost of your ads. You could provide a catering service and write off cookbooks and olive oil. You could start a little network marketing company and enroll clients in the National Audit Defense Network and write off part of the cost of your lunch with prospective clients. All of these and any number of other businesses and expenses are completely legitimate—legal in every respect.

# Chapter Six

# Keys to Starting a Home Business

*"From the tiny acorn...the mighty oak does grow."*
**-Anonymous**

*"There are really two (2) tax systems in this country: one for individuals and one for businesses."*
**-Robert Bennington,**
**President of National Audit Defense Network**

As you begin to conceive ways to set up your home business, there are some critical concepts you need to keep in mind if you want the Internal Revenue Service to recognize your enterprise as a legitimate business. The United States Tax Code which is interpreted by the country's judiciary system, has four basic tenets which you will want to follow. Remember that violating any one of these basic principles of the code is just asking for big trouble. If you ignore or forget one seemingly unimportant aspect of structuring your home business, you will invalidate, in the eyes of the IRS, the entire business. On the other hand, these aspects are not that many in number, and really not very complicated at all. If you do it right from the beginning, you'll save yourself a lot of headaches (and, most likely, money) in the long run. The four basic tenets to follow are:

1) Your business must show an intent to make a profit
2) Your home office must have the primary purpose of running your business
3) You must treat transactions professionally, as a business person would
4) You must document all business-related income and expenses

## Intent to Make a Profit

This is probably the Internal Revenue Service's number one consideration when determining whether or not your business is legitimate. In the simplest terms, you've got to be able to convince the IRS that your business exists for the purpose of making a profit. In the words of the United States Tax Code, can you demonstrate a "profit motive" or "profit objective?" You do not necessarily have to make a profit (see below), but you do have to show that you have made a reasonable attempt to do so. When the IRS auditor comes around, you have to look him or her straight in the face and say, "You know what? I tried as hard as I could to make a profit." Remember, it's not illegal to be a terrible business person and not show a profit, but you need to be able to stand up in front of that auditor and say, "I started this business, and I really, really tried to make a profit. I went out there and I did everything I could to make money." As long as you can honestly and convincingly say that, you are entitled to write off any losses you incurred from the business. You're also entitled to write off all of your legal business expenses.

Keep in mind, as I said, you can be a terrible business person and have a business that no person in his or her right mind, including yourself, would expect to show a profit. That is, there need not be an "expectation of profit." You cannot be faulted, or penalized, for an overly risky venture. You just have to show you tried to make more than you spent.

For example: let's say you decided to start a lawn-maintenance business. You bought a pick-up truck, a John Deere tractor-mower, a trimmer, a blower, rakes, brooms, and hoses. Your business was named, "Manchester Lawn Care." Was that enough to show you tried to make a go at running a legitimate business? Not yet. So far, you hadn't made an honest attempt to make a profit. Question: how is the IRS supposed to know you didn't buy those items for your own personal use, or bought them just to create the illusion that you were running a business?

So, just how do you show an "intent" to make a profit? Well, let's word it a little differently and look at like this: How would you actually try to make money from this "business"? First, you'd let folks know that you are in fact in business. You'd take out ads in the local paper. Perhaps you'd print up some flyers, have business cards made and have a sign painted on the side of your pick-up. Then you would begin keeping records of your expenses, open a bank account in the name of your business, preferably a checking account with "Manchester Lawn Care" written across the top of your checks. And (here's where it gets interesting) you might take some people out to lunch or dinner in an attempt to recruit customers. You might join some business associations or you might attend professional conferences on landscape maintenance where you network with folks in your field and learn about other ways to market yourself. You might buy a computer which would allow you access to online information about types of lawn diseases and fertilizers, and you'd probably want a software program that would more efficiently keep track of your records:  expenses, losses, income, customers' names, addresses, lawn sizes and types, special requests, etc.

All of this could get quite expensive. But don't worry. Remember, I said you don't necessarily have to show a profit, only an attempt to make one.

Generally speaking, the Internal Revenue Service expects you to show evidence of net income three out of every five years. If you don't, they're likely to claim your "business" is just a hobby and that you never intended to show a profit at all. But even if you don't show a profit in that third year, you're not totally sunk; you're just more likely to be targeted by the IRS to justify yourself.  Remember, though, there are huge numbers of legitimate businesses—from pharmaceutical companies to software manufacturers to dot-com firms—that legally show losses for far more than three years in a row.

Nevertheless, the three year figure is good to work with, if for no other reason than it allows you time in which you most likely won't be scrutinized by the IRS and you can show losses without worrying too much about auditors breathing down your neck.

Let's say the first three years Manchester Lawn Care showed losses. You'd only managed to contract with a dozen or so regular customers, and your income was far below your expenses. It's okay. As long as you kept records of everything, including copies of, and receipts for, all your expenses, you're in the clear.  As long as you could show clearly and with documentation that you made every feasible effort to turn a profit, you followed the tax code tenet that your home business had  an "intent" to make a profit.

# Your Office and Its Primary Purpose

The source of much debate in the last quarter century or so has been over exactly what makes a home office a legitimate place of business for the purposes of the Internal Revenue Service. For years, the standard definition (itself continually challenged and reinterpreted) was that your home office had to be your "primary place of business." That is, if you had a hardware store on Broadway, you couldn't then also have a deductible office at home—even if you did a substantial amount of work there—because home wasn't where you conducted your primary business.

In addition, until recently you were required to see clients at your office. Problem: What if your business didn't require that you saw clients there? What if, say, you had a pool service and all the clients you saw were at their homes? In all honesty, why would someone whose pool you service want to stop by your home office, where you keep your records and store your chemicals (which you deliver) and tools (which you bring to the job sites)? In fact, a case in Texas tested this very criterion. A farmer had set up a home office and claimed it as a deduction, but the IRS said, "No, you don't see clients there, so you can't write off your home-office expenses." Thankfully, the farmer was so sure that what he was doing was legal and legitimate that he went to court over it—and he won. The judge recognized that paying bills and other office work was an integral part of the maintenance of a productive farm; the farmer was allowed the write-off.

The third criteria that the IRS used until recently to determine the viability of a home-office deduction was that the office had to exist for the employer's benefit, not yours. That was always an easy one to prove. All you had to do as an employee was get a letter from your boss stating there was no room for you at the main office and that if you wanted to keep your job you were going to have work from home. Case closed.

Thankfully, Congress saw the folly of such definitions and criteria. In 1998 some major changes were made to the Tax Code that directly affect whether or not and to what degree you can claim your home office as a deduction. In most cases, these changes have been for the better of the taxpayer and home-business owner.

First of all, your home office no longer has to be the place where you conduct most of your business. Let's say you're out on the road most of the time. You have a business in which you sell vacuum cleaners and you spend a good portion of your day going door-to-door demonstrating them. Maybe you only spend 5% of your time physically in the office, doing paperwork, accounting, invoicing, etc. Since the newest (at time of print) definition of a home office does not involve an expenditure of time in the office, this is still a legitimate deduction—and one allowed by the Tax Code, not one you're going to have fight for in court. So the question to ask to determine whether your home office is allowable as a deduction is not, "Is it my primary place of business?" but, "Is it used for the exclusive purpose of my business?" In the case of the vacuum-cleaner salesman, he might have only been in that office 5% of the time, but that office was set up and used exclusively for making his business (more) profitable and professional.

Another key consideration is the ownership of the building. Don't think that just because you don't own the premises in which you have set up your office that you can't claim a home-office deduction. As a renter, you can just as legitimately and legally claim that deduction. For example, here at the National Audit Defense Network, we lease the office space that we're in, and we still get to claim the deduction for the lease payments because they're part of the cost of doing business.

Set-up of your home office is simple. Whether it is full-time or just a sideline that may one day become a full-time business, you have many options available to you. Of course, I believe that setting up an MLM operation is not only the easiest, but most profitable, if you find the right venture. Other options include turning an expensive hobby, such as photography, into a money-making venture. Your home-based business need not generate your major source of income; it is essential, however, that you demonstrate your intention of making a profit.

It is essential to keep accurate records of your income and expenses—even if your business generates a loss. The IRS has the option to disallow ALL your expenses if they find faulty records regarding ANY of your expenses—this has continually been found in favor of the IRS in the courts. Remember, the IRS's attitude has always been that people try and cheat on their taxes, therefore, if they can find an expense deduction that you can't document, they will assume you are trying to cheat. Penalties assessed for failure to keep good records are high. If they can find you in error, they can assess you:

- 1/2 of 1% per month of the amount they have assessed you underpaid as a failure to pay penalty for every month they feel you have owed them
- 20% of the amount they have assessed you underpaid as punishment for negligence or disregard of the rules, or because they claim you did not have reasonable basis for

the deduction, or if there is a substantial understatement of tax

- 75% of the underpayment if they feel they can prove fraud.

Now, don't get scared off from the idea of starting your home based business; that's just what the IRS would like to see. Just understand why I stress the importance of building a documentation system—more of which will be discussed later.

## Treat All Transactions Professionally

Treat transactions as a business person would. In addition to maintaining your intent to make a profit and defining your office space within the parameters established by the Internal Revenue Service, you simply need to treat all transactions professionally and with the integrity and respectability expected in the business world. This includes everything from providing prospective customers with written estimates of work to be done to follow-up phone calls regarding customer satisfaction. It includes maintaining separate bank and checking accounts and using a separate credit card only for business purposes. It includes keeping copies of employee applications and correspondence. It also includes keeping accurate records of income and expenses, ideally with graphs charting your company's growth.

Remember, too, that though oftentimes you might start out doing business with friends (who better to help you get your business off the ground, right?) you still need to keep records and treat the relationships professionally. Even if Manchester Lawn Care's first customers were your in-laws down the street, provide them a written contract, of which you will keep a copy, as well as bills and other records.


## Allowable Business Expenses


As you would expect, the Internal Revenue Service has very strict guidelines for determining exactly which types of business expenses are deductible and which aren't. According to Section 162 of the United States Tax Code, deductions are allowed for:
"all the ordinary and necessary expenses paid or incurred during the taxable year for carrying on a trade or business."

I say "strict guidelines," but you can see that there's certainly some room for interpretation. The key is you are able to make a case that the expense is connected to your profit motive or profit objective. Obviously, for example, what is "ordinary and necessary" for one person's business wouldn't be for another. While a general contractor might be able to write off the cost of a new table saw, the owner of a pest-control service wouldn't. *Remember:* "ordinary and necessary" is defined within the context of the business or trade you are conducting. In Chapter 8, I'll go over in detail many of the deductions that, as the owner of a small business you'll be able to claim. For now, you can see that the list includes some rather convenient and attractive ones. For example: your home, or parts thereof, your car or other vehicle, a percentage of meals, travel, entertainment are all deductible as long as they meet the criteria of being "ordinary and necessary." This could mean anything from a computer for electronic billing to new windows in your rental property could be deductible.

Remember that you are not allowed to deduct personal, family, or living expenses. In most cases, you can draw a clear line between personal expenses and business expenses. In some cases, however, an expense might be part business and part personal, as in the case of a home repair when the home contains an allowable home office. In that case, a percentage of the expense will be deductible, based on the percentage of the home that is being used as an office. It's also important to remember that some expenses are not "divisible." For example, if you start a company and use your existing telephone to conduct business, you cannot deduct the percentage you use for your company. If you want to deduct telephone expenses, you must get a separate phone and separate line, solely for use by your business. Though this might seem inconvenient (and perhaps even unnecessary considering how you run your business) it can actually work in your favor. Phones are cheap, and so are additional lines; your long-distance calls would cost you the same amount on either line. In this regard, this is an inexpensive way to demonstrate the viability of your business. It effectively shows the government that you are, in fact, taking your enterprise seriously, you're making every effort to be professional and, in so doing, maintaining your profit objective.

## Demonstrating the Viability of Your Business

Because your recently established home business is just that—recently established—the first time you file your income taxes as an owner of that business, you'll be sending up a red flag that virtually says "Come and get me." Let's say for the past eight years, you and your spouse have been filing basic 1040 forms. Each time your return was subject to the complex human and computer mechanisms of the IRS—designed precisely to identify aberrations—everything went fine. It all went without a hitch. Suddenly however, you've got something new: a home business with deductions, expenses, exclusions, maybe even losses! This, of course, required you to include new forms and perhaps enlist the assistant of a CPA or other tax professional. Red alert! Red alert! That's right, your changes were noted. Now that doesn't necessarily mean things will grind to a halt at the IRS as clerks and agents gather round a computer to see what you're up to. However, eyebrows will rise and there will be sly glances across desktops, and while your chances of being audited remain low, you just increased them; it's wise to be prepared.

What I'm going to offer you now are some of the questions that the IRS would ask you in order to determine whether or not your home business is viable. Anticipate these questions, and conduct your business accordingly. Be prepared to answer the questions clearly and with documentation, and you should be in good stead. Legal and Legitimate!

### 1. Did you conduct your business in a professional and business-like manner?

This one's pretty straightforward, really, and is fairly easy for you to answer, assuming you've kept receipts and records as I've been imploring you to do all along. Essentially, could you demonstrate that you didn't co-mingle funds? That is, did you have separate bank accounts for your business and your personal use? You wouldn't want to write a check for a new rake for your lawn-care business on the same account that you write a check for your new golf clubs. Neither would you want to pay a bill for your business telephone on the same account that you paid a bill for your home telephone. Keep in mind that there are some fabulous accounting programs that you can buy for your computer for not much more than $100 on which you can easily and professionally keep records. You might also discuss this angle with your accountant or tax professional and ask him for other suggestions. Keeping a log of your conversations is also a good idea.

*Note:* if you intend to do business using any other name than your own (even if your name is John Alden and you company is to be called "John Alden Public Speaking Consultants"), most localities require you to file a DBA ("Doing Business As") certificate. This generally includes simply providing your full name and address and then indicating the name under which you will do business. In some areas, you are also required to provide notice in a local newspaper: "John Alden of 2 Standish Street is hereby doing business as John Alden Public Speaking Consultants." You might be required to run this notice for a specific number of days or editions of the newspaper.

**2. Did you keep satisfactory records?**

As will be discussed in great detail in the next chapter, this is one of the most important aspects of determining the viability of your enterprise. Keep all your receipts; keep them in order, either in monthly envelopes (which is my favored method), or by some of other method of your own design. And keep a log, indicating how those expenses were relevant to your business.

**3. How have you worked to improve the profitability of your business?**

Like most of the questions you're going to be asked, this one is completely fair. If you think about it, it is a question you should be asking yourself anyway. Have you attempted to enlist new clients/customers? Have you attended seminars learning about how to market your product? Have you met with suppliers and wholesalers in an attempt to decrease your costs? All of these are ways not only to increase the profitability of your business but, for the purposes of the IRS, specific ways to convince them you've made that attempt. Ideally, you'll sit down with your auditor and without hesitation say, "Let me tell you about the eight things I did this year to increase the profitability of my business."

**4. What are your qualifications for being in this business?**

Again, this is another easy question, as long as you believe in yourself—because this is where you sell yourself. A legitimate answer would be, "Well, I like to make money, and selling this product makes me feel good. My grandmother started taking this vitamin, and she's in better shape right now than Venus Williams. I want to share that with people and make money doing so." You could also say, "Well, I've been in this field for six years and it fascinates me." Basically, you just have to tell them why you love your business.

**5. What improvements are you making in the business to increase profitability?**

This question is very much like #3 above, and there could be some overlapping; you might want to answer with discussions of your inventory, for example, or your tools. Perhaps you upgraded your software to keep better records of your clients' individual needs. Perhaps you painted your old pick-up to present to potential customers a more professional appearance and, in so doing, created a larger client base. Perhaps you took a class that licensed or certified you to take on larger and more complex projects.

In a nutshell, then, you simply have to make a case that you're doing what any reasonable business person would do in trying to make a go of his or her enterprise. *Remember:* you need not show a profit, particularly at first. Even if you're showing losses year after year (even past the three-year point, after which the IRS would like to see you making money) you still have a good chance of convincing them that your deductions are legitimate.

## Last-Minute Considerations

Of course, year in and year out you're keeping an open eye for legal and legitimate deductions. You save your receipts, keep your logs, and hope that what you end up with will decrease your tax liability to a degree that both you and the government will find satisfactory. All too often however, as the end of the year approaches, you find yourself scrambling, trying to find one last good-sized deduction—a contribution, a business expense, etc. Well, here's one that most folks (even a lot of accountants and other tax professionals) don't even know exists.

You can elect to treat the cost of your purchase of any depreciable assets that you use in your business, company, or trade, as an expense rather than a capital expenditure. The section 179 election allows you to expense up to $24,000 of the cost of equipment in the year you purchase it rather than having to depreciate it over a number of years. Now, there are exceptions here, so don't get too excited yet. For example, you can't take that large of a deduction for an automobile that you've purchased. However, if you've got an electrical contracting company and you bought a van or truck whose gross weight totals 6,000 pounds or more and you use that vehicle solely for your business, you can take advantage of that full $24,000 deduction in the year 2002! Keep in mind, too, that you only need to use that vehicle one day of that year—and it can certainly be December 31st—for it to qualify.

# Chapter Seven

# Document
# EVERYTHING

*"For a man with a firm grasp of his intentions, neither the heated passions of his fellow-citizens...nor the face of a tyrant...will shake him in his firm based mind."*
**-Horace,** *Epistles*

*"What is all knowledge too but recorded experience?"*
**-Thomas Carlyle,** *On History*

Though keeping meticulous business records can at times seem to be too much bother, in the long run it's more than worth it. When push comes to shove, no matter how legitimate your "profit objective" is, no matter how justified your home office is, if you can't prove it all with documentation, then all your hard work (and deductions) just go up in smoke. Should the Internal Revenue Service get you in their sights, your records will make all the difference. If you've done everything right and you can prove it, it's more than likely that you'll come out on the back end of an audit without owing either any additional taxes or having to pay any penalties.

I'm going to ask for 30 seconds a day of your time. If you can commit to just 30 seconds a day, I'll show you how you can keep records that will satisfy even the most picky and vengeful of auditors. Thirty seconds a day doesn't sound like much, but you'd be surprised how many people either forget to take that time or just never get around to it.  So when they get audited, they're either completely empty-handed or their records are in such chaos that they're effectively useless. Imagine for a moment that your boss comes up to you and says, "I'm going to give you a raise; a raise of three, four, or five thousand dollars. All you have to do is spend an extra 30 seconds here at the office." Now, who in her right mind wouldn't say yes to that in a heartbeat?  And who in her right mind wouldn't follow through and stay those 30 extra seconds every day, and wear a big ol' grin the whole time?

I'm going to offer that exact same raise, but you've got to commit to those 30 seconds. Let me start by giving you some examples of how you can spend that time in such a way that, if the IRS were to audit you, you'd come through with flying colors. First of all, I always tell my clients to develop a simple system by which they can keep track of all their receipts. This is *absolutely critical*, and not at all complicated. This is what I do; I suggest you do something along the same lines.  During the course of the day (and believe me, I'm not the most organized guy in the world) I just shove all my business receipts into my pockets. Then when I come home, the very first thing I do before I hug my kids, pet my dog or kiss my wife, is to walk over to a manila envelope that I keep ten feet from my front door.  Into that envelope, I simply empty my pockets of all the receipts collected that day. Then I go and hug my kids, kiss my wife, take off my coat, and consider myself home from work. At the end of each month, I seal up the envelope, put it away somewhere safe, and put out a new one.

Why do I do this? Because it is a way I can effectively and efficiently keep track of each month's receipts. If I ever get audited, and the IRS agent says to me, "All right, I want to see the receipts of that trip you took in December 1999 when you took the shuttle from your home to the airport, rented that car, went to dinner at...," I just pull out my envelope, and say, "Here you go, Sir."

The second critical aspect of documenting your business is keeping a log. It's very important that you keep a log for the deductions you take for your meals, entertainment, travel, and many other expenses. Keep in mind, too, that the IRS requires you make your entries in your log within 24 hours of incurring the expense. So, simply make it a part of your everyday routine; before you sit down for dinner, after dinner, before you go to bed. It doesn't matter when you do it as long as you develop the routine. Just as you brush your teeth every day, sit down with your log and pen and make those entries. Once you get into the routine, it won't take you more than 20 or 25 seconds, and there, coupled with the five seconds it takes to drop your receipts into an envelope, are your 30 seconds a day! Then, when the Internal Revenue Service checks your receipts, and you've got them properly filed, and then they check your logs, and they're properly done, well, there's really nowhere else for them to go. You'll be looking very, very good. *Remember:* The IRS requires that you log your entries within 24 hours of incurring the expense.

This strategy may sound too simple, but it works. This is why: each IRS agent has dozens of cases on his desk at any given time. It's nothing personal with you; he or she doesn't want your money any more than they want anyone else's money. As long as you have meticulous documentation, your IRS auditor is quickly going to realize that he or she will not be able to generate much additional revenue from you.  Now, the IRS claims that they don't promote their agents according to how productive they are in terms of generating additional revenue dollars, but let's face the facts.  The IRS is, in fact, a collection agency, and they are charged with getting the most tax money from you as possible.

If you're a tough target, and the other nine cases on the agent's desk are less challenging, then you know which return will be left alone. If the agent knows that the next person to walk into the office will have their receipts in a ripped-up shopping bag, have no log of his expenses, and be more nervous than a crippled fawn with a pack of wolves circling in for the kill, imagine her glee as dollar signs and promotions appear in her eyes. "Come right in," she'll say, rubbing her palms together. In other words, by keeping your receipts in order, and by keeping a professional log, you lower the amount of desire she can even muster up to work on your case.

## Find A Method That Works For You

I've summarized the way in which I keep my own business records, but I fully understand that my method won't work for everyone. The key is to find a method or system that will work for you.  There are certain things to keep in mind no matter what your method. For example, in addition to keeping your receipts and a daily log, you should also keep a systematic and easily retrievable set of professional files. You might set aside a drawer in a file cabinet specifically for this purpose and then keep a folder for each type of record.

A colleague of mine recently hired his two daughters to do

some work for him. Their payment, which he deducts from his overall tax liability, is easy to justify because he has used his filing system to keep track of the process. He's filed a copy of his "Help Wanted" sign, which he posted on their bedroom doors, the resumes and cover letters his daughters submitted to him, his notes from their interviews, and, probably most importantly, their time sheets and records of work done and money paid to them.

A couple of other record-keeping strategies to consider: If your bank offers you the option of returning your cancelled checks to you, take advantage of this. That way, you can staple the check to the receipt, or, if you don't have the receipt, the cancelled check itself can serve as the receipt. It's also a good idea to keep a separate credit card for your business; each month, after you pay the bill, file your itemized statement. This will go a long way toward both establishing the legitimacy of your business (for IRS purposes) and toward keeping a clean track record of your expenses (for your own purposes).

In addition to official paperwork for your business, there are a handful of other things you can keep in your file that could very well help you provide documentation later on, should you need it. Photographs are natural (and very convincing) form of documentation. A nice set of photos is a great way to document, for example, a home office conversion; one picture showing the "before," one showing work in progress, one showing the "after." You can also keep track of simple improvements to your office that way, an added window, for example. Or, say you have a pool service, you can keep photographic records of your customers' pools.

It's also important that you keep your records for a period of time after you have filed your tax return (see below). With this in mind, you're going to need to transfer some of your files each year; I like to have a "Current Year" drawer, and then a simple manila envelope for preceding calendar years. I write the year on the outside of the envelope, seal it up, and put it on the top shelf of the closet in my office. If I don't need it after six years, I toss it. If I do end up needing it, there it is.

## Hang on to Past Years' Records

As Shelley wrote way back in 1822, "The world is weary of the past," and by the time you've filed your taxes, so are you. The calendar year is long over; April 15 has come and gone—you met the deadline without even breaking a sweat! Maybe you even received a nice little refund check from the IRS. If the refund check was rather large, that means you overpaid the government all year and need to change your strategy. I always figure that if the amount I either pay or get back is under $100, I've done a good job of tax planning.

Needless to say, you'll also have several drawers full of last year's files, receipts, and log books. It may be awful tempting to toss them out, but don't!    It's absolutely critical that you keep everything—at least for a little while longer.

The length of time you must hang on to your records varies, but a good general rule of thumb is this three years. This is based on Section 6501(a) of the tax code: "The amount of any tax imposed... shall be assessed within 3 years after the return was filed (whether or not such return was filed on or after the date prescribed)." That means in most cases you need to keep records for at least three years after you file. I say "at least" because although it's always nice to clean out closets and throw out useless paperwork, your records actually take up very little space. If you can find a place to store them for a little longer, well, it can't hurt.

There are some exceptions (naturally!). For one, if you made a purchase of an asset that you continue to use in your business, then you must keep the records of that purchase for the entire time that asset is in your possession, plus the three years stipulated above. Also, if you file and fail to include 25% or more of your income, then you are liable for six (6) years after filing. Finally, if you fail to file altogether, file a falsified claim, or otherwise willfully "attempt to evade filing," then "a proceeding in court for collection of such tax may be begun without assessment, *at any time.*"

**Extensions:** thankfully, the IRS allows for extensions of the due dates for your filing. These can come in handy in a number of ways.

# What Happens If You Don't Keep Records

The range of things that can happen to you if you don't keep business records is sweeping. Of course, nothing at all might happen. It's quite possible that the Internal Revenue Service will never take notice of your little enterprise. You could perhaps go on for years, blithely claiming deductions for which you have no documentation, without one single raised (IRS) eyebrow.

At the other extreme, you could be liable for penalties that might effectively cost you your business. Basically, since your documentation is all you have to establish the legitimacy of your business, your company could be deemed a hobby if you can't prove otherwise. Remember that the burden of proof is on you, not on the IRS. Remember too, failing to report income constitutes tax fraud— a situation with no statute of limitations. Since the burden of proof is always on the taxpayer, the IRS could conceivably come to you ten years down the road and claim that you didn't file in such and such a year; if you have no records you could be technically guilty of tax fraud.

First of all, not keeping your receipts could simply cost you the deductions to which you're legally entitled. Suppose you bought a new router that you use exclusively for your woodworking business. Didn't keep the receipt? Sorry! It's not a deductible expense if you couldn't prove what you paid for it and when. But compared to being fined, you got off easily. According to Section 6662(a) of the United States Tax Code, in the case of underpayment: "an amount equal to 20 percent of the portion of the underpayment shall be added to" the amount you owe. Among the reasons for underpayment are the following:

(1) Negligence or disregard of rules or regulations; and

(2) Any substantial understatement of income tax.

"Negligence'" is defined in the code as "any failure to make a reasonable attempt to comply with the provisions of this title, and the term ''disregard" includes any "careless, reckless, or intentional disregard."

In addition, according to Section 6663(a) of the tax code, if you willfully attempt in "any manner to evade or defeat any such tax or the payment thereof (you) shall, in addition to other penalties provided by law, be liable for a penalty of 75 percent of the total amount of the underpayment of the tax."

Finally, there's also the consideration of interest. That's

right. The government charges interest on the money you owe. Let's say the return being audited is for five years ago. Because of missing receipts, the IRS disallows a substantial amount of the expenses you claimed resulting in you being assessed an amount as "underpayment." On top of the initial amount of the underpayment goes the penalties, and on top of all that goes five years worth of interest. It's not unusual for $800 in missing receipts to turn into a $4,000 tax bill.

I'm not stressing this to discourage you from taking those deductions. On the contrary, my motto is: take all the deductions the law allows! I simply want you to know why I suggest that even if the law only requires you to keep your records for three years, keep them longer anyway.

# Chapter Eight

# Miscellaneous Business Deductions

*"I must Create a System, or be enslav'd by another Man's."*
**-William Blake, *Jerusalem***

*"Were it not for the imagination, Sir, a man would be as happy in the arms of a chambermaid as of a Duchess."*
**-Samuel Johnson, letter to James Boswell**

As I've said elsewhere in this book, the best thing you can do to reduce your tax liability is to take advantage of as many deductions and credits as you legally can. To a degree, the deductions you can take are limited only by your imagination. Almost every day I talk to people who are surprised at the number of deductions available to them. Whether it's hiring family members to work for you, going out to lunch with prospective customers, or going to a conference in Cleveland, you can write off all or portions of almost all of your business-related expenses.

As a general rule, deductible expenses are those that are "ordinary and necessary" in the maintenance of your business—those that help you initiate or maintain the company's profit objective. If on the trip to Cleveland you spent at least 50% of your time learning more about your field, or attempting to recruit new clients, then you've got yourself some legitimate deductions. The key is to learn to work those purchases, trips, and lunches within the parameters allowed by the Internal Revenue Service. If you do, and you meticulously document the proceedings, then you should be in the clear; if you are ever audited, you should come out smelling like a rose.

## Deducting A Portion of Your Home

One of the best ways to reduce your tax liability is to operate your business out of your home. By doing so, you can write off not only all of the expenses related to the office you maintain in that home, but you can also write off appropriate percentages of other home-related expenses. For example, suppose you make your own candles and have a mail-order distribution service. Certainly you need a place in your home to make the candles, and you probably also need a room set aside for record keeping. You can calculate the percentage of the home's square footage that you use for your business (assuming you use it exclusively for that purpose—see Chapter 6) and use that number to figure many different deductions. Let's say your home's square footage totals 2,000 square feet; the candle-making room measures 15 feet by 12 feet (180 feet), and the room you use for the office measures 10 feet by 12 feet. That totals 300 square feet you're using for your business, or 15% of your home's total.

Now you can use that number to figure any number of deductions. First of all, if you rent the home in which you've established your office, you can deduct the portion of your monthly rent that is attributable to your home office. If you own your home, on the other hand, you can deduct or depreciate proportionately appropriate percentages of purchase costs as well as expenses and home improvements. For example, let's say you painted the exterior of your home this year to the tune of $4,000. Using our earlier example, you could legally deduct 15% or $600 of that cost. Additionally, you can write off a percentage of the cost of your homeowner's insurance, your utility bills, including those for gas and electricity used for heating and air conditioning, as well as water, sewer, and garbage pick-up costs.

Keep in mind that if you are going to deduct the expense of the telephone you use for your business, you must have a separate business line from that which you use for personal reasons. The IRS and courts have been wrestling with this one for years. While it might be legal to deduct the cost of, say, a long-distance business call that you make on your personal line, you're better off just keeping a separate line. This is not only inexpensive but also helps to establish your sincerity as someone making every attempt to operate a professional business.

Naturally, 100% of the cost of furniture, equipment, and supplies that you use for your office can be written off. Office supplies such as a box of paper clips and furniture like file cabinets or a couch for your clients qualify for this deduction. However, depending on their costs, purposes, and life span, you might have to depreciate them. Your accountant can help you determine which expenses you can write off directly and which you will need to depreciate.

Finally, you can also deduct the cost of services required to maintain your home. For example, if you have a pest-control company that comes out monthly and sprays under your eaves, you can deduct the appropriate percentage for that service. If you have a house cleaner whom you pay $75 a week, you can deduct the appropriate percentage of the $3,900 a year you pay her—after all, she does clean your office, doesn't she?

Note that some services will or won't be deductible depending on the kind of business you own. For instance, if you have a business which requires that clients visit your home office, you might be able to deduct the cost of your pool service, as a pool full of leaves and algae does not look very good and would reflect on the professional image you are trying to project . However, let's say you're a travel writer and all your contact with editors and publishers is through the mail and telephone. In that case, it's unlikely you'd be able to make a case that maintaining your pool is "ordinary and necessary" for the profit objective of your business. On the other hand, the IRS has allowed the monthly service fee for a home-security system to be deducted and has granted depreciation allowance for the cost of the system.

Another expense of which you can take advantage is that of traveling between your home office and the places where you actually do your work. Let's come back to the example of the lawn-care business. Your job sites—where you do a large percentage of your work—would actually be away from your office, the site where you do your billing, keep your records, order supplies, etc. Remember, your office no longer needs to be your "principal place of business." As long as the office is used exclusively for the purposes of conducting business, it's deductible, and so then are the costs of traveling from it to job sites.

Finally, keep in mind that like everything else related to your home business, you must document the fact that you are using a specific portion of your home for that purpose. It's a good idea to have blueprints that specify the area of your home that you're using. If that's impossible, get some draft paper and do a drawing yourself of the arrangement. Also, take some photos: close-ups of your desk, computer, file cabinets, and copy machine, as well as long shots of the entire office area. Maybe even get someone to take a picture of you sitting at your desk at work. Then, along with all your other records, put your drawings and photos in a place where you can easily retrieve them should you need to establish proof of the legitimacy of your home office.

# Deducting Your Vehicle

Whether you use your personal vehicle for your business or you've purchased a vehicle specifically and exclusively for use in your business, you are entitled to certain deductions of which you should take advantage. The IRS allows not only for the cost of driving your car (fuel purchases, etc.) but also for the cost of maintaining it in good working good order, and also allows for "normal wear and tear." In declaring your deduction, you can choose between itemizing your expenses (and deducting that total) or calculating your expenses based on the IRS-established mileage rate.

Currently, the IRS mileage rate is 36.5 cents per mile, plus costs of parking, tolls, etc. This allowance is intended to cover everything from insurance to new tires to mechanical tune-ups and gasoline. The IRS figures that 36.5 cents per mile ought to cover the whole shebang.

They also figure people will prefer to take the easy way. As we all know, however, the easy way is not always the best way. Instead of itemizing your expenses, keeping track of all your maintenance costs, and saving all your gas receipts, you can simply take the total number of miles you drive and multiply it by .365. If you drove 15,000 miles in a given year, you could deduct $5,475. That definitely is easy, but does that amount equal the amount you'd spend on maintaining the vehicle? Don't be so sure.

In fact, one of the major rental car companies recently reported that their actual cost of operating an average mid-sized automobile was actually 65 cents per mile. Think about this for a minute. They buy and service their vehicles in quantity guaranteeing lower cost. They buy their gas at discount rates and have their own mechanics. Yet it still costs them 65 cents per mile to operate those vehicles.

Take away those discounts and the truth is, the amount you and I pay to operate a vehicle is closer to a dollar per mile. The nice thing is, you do have a choice; if you're not sure which method is best for you, do the following to find out:  just keep track of those expenses. Stash a manila envelope under the front seat of your car, and then every time you buy gas, have the oil changed, replace your windshield wipers, buy air freshener—whatever—just reach down and pop that receipt into the envelope. Then every month or so, take the envelope out, put it somewhere safe, and stash a new one under the seat.  At the end of the year, add up all those receipts. Then include the amount you've paid for car insurance and other miscellaneous expenses, and see if doesn't total more than the generous IRS allowance of 36.5 cents per mile

.

# Deducting Meals

Writing off parts of your meals, taking and arranging, trips to exotic locales is one of the best parts of having your own business. Imagine going out to a nice restaurant, having a cocktail, ordering steak and lobster, a bottle of wine, and then crème brulèe for dessert—and then writing off half the meal.  Imagine taking a business trip to Hawaii, luxuriating in a nice hotel on Maui's west shore, doing a little snorkeling, playing a round of golf, taking in a luau, and enjoying moonlight strolls on the beach.

All of this can be yours on a business trip at a fraction of what it would cost if you were to do it purely for pleasure.  Does that sound too good to be true?   Well, it's not—if you play by the rules and, as always, keep records demonstrating how it all ties into your business.

Let's talk about meals first. Section 274 of the Tax Code allows you to take a client out to lunch and write off 50% of the cost of that meal—including both food and beverages.   The only restriction is that the purpose of the meal is to initiate a new, or nurture an existing, business relationship. Let me tell you a little story, and you'll see just one way to get legally creative with your meals and meetings so that you can write parts of them off as business expenses.

My mother lives in the same city as I do, and loves to play bingo. She's also very proud of my work that I do through National Audit Defense Network.  In fact, when she plays bingo, she tells anyone sitting near her all about National Audit Defense Network, and she's very excited about it. Of course, her excitement becomes contagious and her fellow bingo players get excited about it too.  So every week when she plays bingo, she collects names, addresses, and phone numbers of people who say that it sounds like an interesting company; and of course, that's information that would be useful to me.

So every single week, sometimes more frequently, I take my mother to lunch. When we sit down, I say to her, "Hey, Mom, have you run into anyone lately who might be interested in the National Audit Defense Network?" Sure enough, out comes her list: the names, addresses, and phone numbers of all the people she's spoken with at her bingo games. What am I doing? I'm soliciting new clients. I'm establishing the business purpose of my lunch with my mother.

Now generally, taking your mother to lunch would not qualify as a legitimate business expense. However, because my mother is giving me leads of potential clients, leads which, obviously, I follow up on, I'm actually able to deduct 50% of the cost of those meals from my overall tax liability.

If you have a home-based business (whether you sell vitamins, water softeners or decide to get involved with the National Audit Defense Network like I am), you take friends or acquaintances out to a meal and ask them if they've run into anyone who might be interested in your business. You have a discussion about those possibilities—then you have a legitimate business expense. You can write off 50% of the cost of that meal. It should go without saying, however, that you cannot deduct the cost of a meal you eat alone unless you're on a business trip—more about that below.

Now I've been having some fun with all this, but I need to stress that what I'm talking about are legal business expenses, deductions you can take with a clear conscience. The Internal

Revenue Service—your fellow taxpayer, actually—is picking up part of the tab for the purposes of helping you establish, maintain, or increase the profit objective of your company. That is in the government's best interest because healthy small businesses help promote a healthy national economy. Naturally, the IRS has determined guidelines that define the parameters of business meals that are deductible, and they're actually not only quite easy to stay within, but are also quite fair.

First of all, you must discuss business at some point during the meal. That includes before or after eating as well. For example, you might want to take care of business over a pre-dinner drink, before digging into that pile of ribs. You might want to wait until dessert, when your potential customer or client is properly fed by the wonderful meal to which you're treating him. The timing doesn't matter as long as a business discussion occurs sometime over the course of the meal. Second, the setting must be one in which a business discussion can effectively transpire. You might have a hard time, for example, making a case that you could carry on a productive sales pitch during a Friday afternoon happy hour with a local band belting out its rendition of the Kinks' "Sunny Afternoon" ("The tax man's taken all my dough..."). Yet the back patio of a nice restaurant specializing in northern-Italian cuisine, where water tumbles into fountains under a grapevine terrace, would be an ideal setting.

Keep in mind that the Tax Code specifies that the meeting should be arranged specifically for the purpose of doing business. That is, if you happen to run into a potential customer at lunch, and pick up her tab, then that isn't going to cut it. If you do run into a situation like that, set up a date for another time. Keep it on the up-and-up, and you won't be put on the defensive later. ***Remember:***

deductible meals must have the purpose of initiating a new, or nurturing an existing, business relationship.

As with any expense that you plan to deduct from your overall tax liability, you need to keep records of your meetings with your business meals. The good news is that the minimum amount of the cost of a meal for which you must keep a receipt is $75. If the amount is anything under that, you need not have a receipt. Remember though, as I said in Chapter 7, it is far better to over document than to under document. If you have receipts for meals under $75, keep them and file them along with all the rest. Even more important than keeping your receipts in the case of expenses for business meals, is keeping your log accurate and up-to-date. Remember that the IRS policy is that you must make your entry in your log within 24 hours of incurring the expense. So, before you go to bed the day in which you incurred that business meal expense, take your log and enter into it all the pertinent information. That information should include:

1. Name of your client, or potential client
2. Place where the meal took occurred
3. Specifics as to what was discussed, particularly in terms of developing your company's productivity and effectiveness—in short, establishment that the purpose of the meal/meeting was directly related to your company's profit objective

Follow these important guidelines and you will never go afoul with the IRS.

# Deducting Entertainment

One true benefit of operating a small business is deducting expenses for entertainment—both at home and on business trips. Once again, you must be able to prove that the entertainment expense is directly related to the profit objective of your business. Taking a client to the theater, golfing, or even on vacation to a remote fishing lodge are examples of the range of legitimate entertainment expenses. The Internal Revenue Service allows 50% of the expenses incurred. Either or both of the following requirements must be met to qualify as legally deductible entertainment expenses:

1. The entertainment must precede or follow a legitimate business meeting; ideally, it should be one that has had substantial effect on your company.
2. The entertainment must be arranged for the purpose of conducting business.

An example of the first requirement would be a trip to a nightclub following the signing of a contract by a new client. Let's say you sell home-security systems. You spent a good portion of the morning at the home of a prospective client, taking measurements and discussing with him his particular needs. Then he not only bought a system, but signed up for a one year of service with your company. A legitimate business expense in that case would be to treat him to a round of golf, even if no further business discussion transpired.

An example of the second requirement would be a meeting with the same prospective client, except this time the discussion about the square footage of his home and his needs for a security system took place on the golf course. In this case, again, the green fees would be deductible.

Here's a little-known angle to writing off entertainment expenses: let's assume you have season tickets or passes to something such as your local pro football team's home games, a theater or symphony, a museum, etc. The IRS views each visit to these places separately. Let's say you spent $1,000 on those football tickets, which bought you two tickets to ten games. Five of the times you attended games you brought clients—an expense of $500. You now have a decent-sized write-off: $250, or 50% of $500.

Finally, remember that similar to meal expenses, you only need to keep receipts for those entertainment costs over $75. For instance, if your green fees totaled $50, you wouldn't be required to file the receipt, although you would need to enter a record of the expense in your log, indicating the date, the client's name, and specifically what business was discussed.

# Deducting Travel

Perhaps the most interesting deduction is that of writing off travel expenses. You can plan deductible trips specifically for the purpose of your business, as well as combine deductible business trips with vacations. Section 162 of the Tax Code allows for "traveling expenses (including amounts expended for meals and lodging other than amounts which are lavish or extravagant under the circumstances) while away from home in the pursuit of a trade or business."

Business travel is defined as a trip for the benefit of your business on which you must spend the night away from your own home. If you don't spend the night, you can't write the entire trip off, only part of it. That is, if you fly to Los Angeles from San Francisco and return the same day, you will be allowed to deduct transportation expenses only, not "on-the-road" expenses (see Travel Expenses in the next section). The only types of business trip whose expense you can't write off are those to seminars or conventions for the purposes of investment. In other words, you couldn't write off a trip to Martinique for the purpose of attending an investment seminar there.

Not very long ago I took a trip to the Bahamas to do a presentation in front of 400 people. Of course, when I got there, in addition to my business obligations, there were other attractions of which I wanted to take advantage: a tour of the island, a boat ride, nightclubs. Basically my trip was just like any other tourist's trip to the Bahamas with one exception: mine was 100% deductible. Why? Because I was on a business trip; any time you're on a business trip, even if you're doing lots of fun stuff, the trip is deductible. In fact, in addition to the three-day seminar itself, I legally counted the day it took to get to the Bahamas and the day it took to get home as part of my travel expenses, and also deducted the expenses I incurred en route.

Of course, again, it's got to be done right; you've got to stay within the parameters established by the Tax Code and by the relevant court cases. If you do that, come April 15, you can claim good-sized and hugely beneficial deductions. You need to spend 50% of your time working. I was at a three-day seminar and spent over half my time working there. The few hours I took to enjoy the area while I was there did not mean I was outside the parameters established by the IRS for business-travel deductions.

Another example:   Let's say every summer you and the family have gone to visit Grandma and Grandpa in Tennessee. Generally speaking, the cost of a visit to the grandparents would not be deductible.    But, let's assume you've started a home-based business of selling vitamins.  If you went to Tennessee and did some presentations, looked for new sources of supplies, or attended a seminar or convention, the purpose of your trip would have been to increase the profitability of your business.  You still saw Grandma and Grandpa, but the trip would, in fact, be deductible.  Bringing your family along, depending on how you travel, would not make the trip any less deductible although you wouldn't be able to deduct their expenses without following certain guidelines.  Let's say you drove to Tennessee keeping in mind that the Internal Revenue Service figures an average normal driving day covers 300 miles. You planned to drive those 300 miles, which would establish the day as a bona fide business day, so your expenses would be deductible.  Obviously, you didn't incur more transportation expenses by having your family along.  Gas, for example, cost the same whether there was one person in your car or four.  So your automobile expenses were deductible, no matter which method you chose to compute them (see "Deducting Your Vehicle).  You also needed a place to stay. If your room rate was the same amount for just yourself as it would for the people with you (many single rooms have two beds), then you could fully deduct that expense as well.  If, on the other hand, there was an added cost for your traveling companions, then you could deduct the cost of your room, less that added rate, and it would still be legal and legitimate. For example, if that hotel or motel charged $75 for a single or double, and charged an extra $10 per person after that, then you could deduct the $75, but not the total $95.

# Two Types of Travel Expenses

When deducting business trip expenses, it's important to keep in mind that the Internal Revenue Service recognizes two distinct types of expenses: transportation expenses, and "on-the-road" expenses.

Transportation includes all the expenses you incur getting to and from your destination: air fare, shuttles, taxis, ferries, etc. All of these expenses are deductible.

"On-the-road" expenses include those you incur on your trip that are germane to simple day-to-day living. Obvious examples include food and lodging, but think about it: What else do you need to do to survive on this planet? You need to wash your clothes. You need to cut your hair. You might need to get your shoes shined for that meeting. The IRS allows 100% deductions for all of these "on-the-road" expenses. The exception is food, for which they allow 50%.

A little-known aspect of this rule is that you can also deduct some "on-the-road" expenses once you return from your trip. For example, of course you might bring along a MacIntosh raincoat on your trip to Dublin. Let's say as you were crossing O'Connell Street on your way to the post office, a taxi splashed mud on you. Naturally, you'd want to get the coat dry cleaned when you got home. That expense, too, would be tax deductible. As long as you can demonstrate that the expense incurred was related to your business trip, you can write if off.

Additionally, there are some quirky rules you need to know about when saving receipts. First of all, as with your food expenses, you only need to keep receipts for expenses that total $75 or more.

That $35 for a taxi ride from your hotel room to the airport doesn't require a receipt. Same with those cassette tapes you bought to record a lecture at a seminar. The quirky thing is that if you weren't on the road, you would have to keep the receipts, and file them away as evidence of those expenses.

The exception to the $75 rule is in the case of lodging. You must keep all hotel and motel receipts, even if you only spent $27 for the executive suite at the Larry, Darryl and Darryl Lodge.

## Hiring Family Members

You can also reduce your tax liability on business trips by hiring family members. You must establish that your spouse and/or kids are legitimately assisting in the conducting of your business, pay them, and deduct that amount. In addition, I said before that you could only deduct, for example, the cost of your motel room for yourself. If, however, the people staying with you are bona fide employees, then you can deduct the cost of their lodging as well. Who qualifies? Anyone who is a legitimate employee of your company, and has a legitimate purpose for joining you qualifies. Let's say you've got a business in which you make custom redwood picnic tables. You go to a woodworkers' convention in Seattle, where there are presentations on design and marketing, and mill reps are discussing various grades of lumber. You wouldn't very well be able to claim as pertinent to your trip your 11-year-old daughter who empties your trash, sweeps the floor of your shop, and cleans off your saws and other tools unless you find legitimate work for her while you're there. If you had her hand out flyers at a trade show, her expenses would then qualify. You could, however, make a very good case for claiming your spouse, who assists you in soliciting new clients, and in purchasing raw materials.

*Note:* Keep in mind that the IRS scrutinizes very closely expenses incurred by employed family members—especially those incurred by your minor children. Also, whether you choose to employ your spouse, or your minor children, remember to keep meticulous records of the number of hours they worked, for whom, what they did, and the dates those activities were performed.

# Chapter Nine

# Choosing Your Business Structure

*"No profit grows where is no pleasure ta' en; in brief,*
*Sir, study what you most affect."*
**-William Shakespeare, *The Taming of the Shrew***

*"A man who has no office to go to - I don't care who he is - is*
*a trial of which you can have no conception."*
**-George Bernard Shaw, *The Irrational Knot***

When Calvin Coolidge told the Society of American Newspaper Editors in 1925 that, "The business of America is business," he meant that it was business that makes this country run, that keeps our economy strong and healthy. For that reason, the government has seen fit to make certain specific attempts to encourage enterprise. The result is that there are far more tax advantages for the business person than there are for the individual. With an individual, the tax rate starts to increase when your income level reaches $6,000—rising very quickly from 10% to 39.1%—while tax on a business stays at 15% until that business has taxable income in excess of $50,000. Obviously, then, if you are an individual who wants to lower your taxes, you need to transform the way you file. You need to become a business person. You need to start a company.

The first step begins with deciding on the structure or form your business venture should take: Sole Proprietorship, Partnership, Limited Liability Corporation, S Corporation or C Corporation. With all the choices available, how do you decide which is the best method to use for the operation of your business?  In making that decision, you may want to look at important factors such as simplicity (or ease of operation), legal protection, and of course tax-saving strategies. For my money, the best kind of company you can start is a C Corporation.  I'll discuss my reasoning about that further on in this chapter.  First though, let's look at the different business structures.

## Sole Proprietorships and Partnerships

The sole proprietorship is the simplest of all business structures. There are, however, distinct drawbacks.  Not the least of these is that you, as an individual, are responsible for liabilities incurred by your company.  In a worst-case scenario, this could include being sued by a customer.  Not only could he take the computer on which you write your cookbooks, but he could also take your car, your house, everything, bankrupting both your company and you personally.

As a Sole Proprietor, you would pay self-employment tax based on your bottom-line Schedule C net income. It would be taxed at individual tax rates rather than corporate rates, which are much lower—especially if your business venture is just starting out and therefore garnering only a small profit. On the other hand, if you have children under 18 and employ them in your business, no Social Security tax would be assessed on their income.

Your medical insurance premiums are not fully deductible with a Sole Proprietorship whereas they may be with a C Corporation. Benefits such as disability insurance premiums and life insurance premiums are not deductible at all under the Sole Proprietorship form of business structure. Of course, if you hire your spouse, you could cover her life insurance and disability insurance premiums. She then can add you on to the policy as her spouse, which is a creative (and legal) way around this restriction.

Partnerships are similar to Sole Proprietorships. The profits and losses of the partnership are passed through to the partners on Schedules K-1 and are taxed on the individual partner's tax returns as ordinary income. The partner's distributive share of partnership ordinary income is subject to self-employment tax on their individual return as are any guaranteed payments made to partners.

## Limited Liability Corporations

Limited Liability Corporations (LLCs) are created and regulated under the laws of each of the individual states. An LLC is allowed to possess the limited liability characteristics of a corporation, but generally has the same options as partnerships for electing tax treatment under the "Check the Box" regulations. This means they can choose their entity classification (i.e., partnership, corporate, sole proprietor, etc.). Federal taxation of LLCs is governed by Subchapter K of the Internal Revenue Code (i.e., Partnership tax law).

Unlike general partners whose personal assets are at risk for claims against the partnership, LLC members are only at risk for their investment in the LLC.  An LLC is nevertheless allowed pass-through taxation, avoiding double-tax on income that is present in corporations.  Combining the benefits of partnership and corporate characteristics, without many of the drawbacks, has created a surge in popularity of Limited Liability Corporations.  As a partnership, the LLC can:

1. Use debt to increase a member's basis
2. Make special allocations of income, gain, loss, deductions and credits
3. Make an Internal Revenue Code (IRC) § 754 election to adjust the basis of LLC assets whenever a member sells his/her membership interest

General partners of partnerships are subject to self-employment tax on their distributive share of partnership income in addition to guaranteed payments. The IRC and Treasury Regulations (TR) do NOT specifically address self-employment tax for LLC members. Therefore, assessment of self-employment tax on LLC members' distributive share of income is unclear.

*A **word of caution:*** Absence of regulations does not necessarily mean LLC distributions are exempt from self-employment tax. Although the IRS presently has no authority under Regulations to assess self-employment tax on an LLC member's distributive share of income, the IRS can try to reclassify amounts as guaranteed payments. If an LLC member receives payments for services, the payments are considered guaranteed payments under the IRC, and as such are subject to self-employment tax. In the absence of regulations, courts must interpret the original intent of Congress when the laws were written, and could reach the same conclusion put forth originally by the proposed regulations.

# The S Corporation

An S Corporation sits somewhere between a sole proprietorship and a full-fledged corporation. That is, the S Corporation enjoys all the legal protection of a regular corporation, with one difference: you as an individual assume the tax liability incurred by your company. All the profits that pass through your S Corporation actually are part of your individual tax return.

This means there is no self-employment tax on your distributive share of and S-corporation's net income. However, as with a Sole Proprietorship, your medical insurance premiums are not 100% deductible (whereas they can be with a C Corporation), and benefits such as Disability insurance premiums and life insurance premiums are not deductible at all.

Many individuals select the S Corporation as their business structure in an effort to avoid "double taxation." By this, I mean that earnings of a C Corporation are taxed at the corporate level and then when distributed to you as dividends, taxed again on your own personal income tax. However, S Corporation earnings flow through to you, so there is no "double taxation" issue. On the other hand, the C Corporation allows for so many benefits that the S Corporation doesn't, that, especially in its early years, avoiding dividend distribution is not that difficult. With no dividend distribution, double taxation is not an issue. Once you've dispensed with that issue, then there is no reason not to give a good, hard look at the C Corporation.

# The C Corporation

As I said at the beginning of this chapter, the C Corporation is my favored structure. Now, I'm sure the image many of you have of a C Corporation includes a 40-story-tall glass office building, 17,000 employees, and $50 million in annual revenues. To be sure, there are C corporations that operate that way, but the vast majority of C Corporations in the United States today are in fact very small companies. And there's no reason whatsoever why you can't start your very own C Corporation and begin almost immediately paying less in taxes.

Incorporating, in general, affords many benefits that will help you reduce your tax liability. The C Corporation however, offers many attractive benefits that other types of corporations, particularly S Corporations, don't. If you recall, the S Corporation acts as a pass through of your profits and, like a sole proprietorship, they are actually part of your individual tax return.

The C Corporation, on the other hand, is its own legal entity, and assumes its own tax liability. You, as operator of a C Corporation, have no personal liability for what that corporation does as long as it's not committing fraud or other egregious acts to violate the rights of other people. That is to say, your C Corporation can run up all sorts of debt, even bankrupt itself, and your personal assets would never be at risk.

For example, a C Corporation affords you ways to avoid paying certain types of taxes—Social Security, for instance—for which you would otherwise be liable. In addition, it provides a way to separate your assets as far as applying for credit goes. Let's say you want to apply for a new-car loan, and, though your personal finances look pretty good, your corporation, albeit temporarily, is in the red. Legally, you need not disclose to your lender your two separate statuses, and in this case you might qualify for a slightly larger loan than if you were required to disclose everything you owned.

Another advantage of operating a C Corporation is that as long as all employees are treated equally (even if you and your spouse are the only ones) you can reimburse yourself for all medical expenses. This includes health-insurance premiums, which constitute a substantial cost and are a perk for which some folks would give their eye-teeth. But that's just the tip of the iceberg. Let's take a look at your entire medical expenses:

In the case of an individual, medical expenses are deductible only to the extent they exceed 7 1/2% of your adjusted gross income and only to the extent you are able to itemize your deductions. Let's say you and your spouse incur $5500 in expenses over the course of the year, for premiums, co-pays, and that Sunday morning visit to clinic. If your adjusted gross income (AGI) is $50,000, the government is only going to let you write c f $1,750 (the amount above 7 1/2% of your AGI.) However, if you're operating a C Corporation you can offer as an employee benefit full compensation for medical expenses to all employees. So your corporation picks up the whole $5500, and then writes off the whole amount as an expense. The government allows corporations to deduct 100% of medical expense benefits. That's right—100%!

Speaking of insurance premiums, still another advantage of a C Corporation is that you can write off group-term life insurance expenses. If you're like most people, you make your money, and from that you pay your 30, 40, or 50% in taxes, and with what little is left over you buy your life insurance policy. Let's say you make $50,000 and pay 30% in taxes; that leaves you $35,000 from which to buy your life insurance, which runs, for the sake of easy math, $1,000 a year. With a C Corporation, all that changes.

If you have a C Corporation, your company policy could be that the corporation picks up the bill for your employees' group-term life insurance policies. Again, as with the medical expenses, 100% of the cost of these premiums is deductible, as long as all your employees are offered the same plan. To keep it simple, let's say your corporation shows a gross profit of $50,000. Your $1,000-a-year life-insurance policy actually decreases the amount for which the corporation would be liable because it's subtracted from that $50,000. So, now you're paying taxes on $49,000 instead of $50,000, and you've already paid for your life-insurance policy. Double your pleasure! As a matter of fact, the government allows corporations to write off up to $50,000 in employee life insurance premiums.

There are, as you would expect, some disadvantages to operating a C Corporation. However, in general, they are not enough to offset the advantages, and in some cases, there are legal ways to decrease their impact. One disadvantage of a C Corporation is that it could put you into a situation of "double taxation" as I mentioned earlier. However, as I also pointed out earlier, there are legal ways to keep the dividends your company pays you to a minimum.

Another thing to watch out for when starting a C Corporation is that if it's defined as a "personal holding" company, A special tax, in addition to regular corporate income tax of 38.6% in 2002 of distributed personal holding company income. However, it is possible to structure even this type of corporation in such a way that you can indeed take full advantage of the C Corporation's many benefits.

# Setting Up a Corporation

Starting up a corporation is much like starting up any new business (see Chapter 6). You need to declare that you are in fact doing business, and you need to do so publicly. Exactly how you do this will depend on where you live as different states and cities have different policies, but you'll probably at least have to take out a "Doing Business As" ad in your local paper. If you're not sure, you can contact a local business association. Most likely, too, you're going to have to pay some fees. In some states you can incorporate for as little as $200—it pays to look around. In fact, you don't even have to incorporate in the state in which you live. Many businesses choose to incorporate in a state such as Nevada that has no corporate taxes, even if they have no intention of ever doing business in that state.

Now, here's where it gets fun if you're starting a C Corporation. Let's say you start your company with an initial $25,000 investment on your part. You could call $20,000 of that a loan that has to be repaid; the remaining $5,000 is stock that would be your own capital investment in your corporation. First of all, there'd be no tax liability on the $20,000 loan because you're simply being repaid the loan. Second, you could pay yourself interest on the $20,000 you paid to the corporation. While you would be subject to the standard tax you'd pay for interest income, that interest would not be subject to Social Security or Medicare tax. This is only one example of excellent strategies to use. The next chapter has many, many more.

# Chapter Ten

# Advanced Tax Strategies for Corporations

"No profit grows where is no pleasure ta'en; in brief, Sir,
study what you most affect."
**-William Shakespeare, *The Taming of the Shrew***

*"The creature has a purpose and his eyes are bright with it."*
**-John Keats, letter, March 19, 1819**

Once you've established a C Corporation, the range of tax advantages will seem limitless. Some of these tax strategies, of course, are more complex than others. Thus I strongly recommend that you consult with a tax professional to see how these and other strategies can best be tailored to suit your individual business needs. Remember, what I'm offering here is an overview; it is not intended to be your ultimate tax guide. That said, let's take a look at several more strategies which you should take advantage of with your new C Corporation.

# Retirement Plans for Corporations

One potential source of substantial savings comes from establishing retirement plans for employees. In fact, if your corporation is netting around $25,000 or more and you don't have some kind of qualified-pension or profit-sharing plan, you're not just missing out each year, you might as well be throwing your hard earned profits away! For example, if your corporation sets up a policy by which you provide significant employee-retirement planning, then the costs of these contributions are deductible from your overall tax liability. You can actually set aside up to 30% of both your income and your employees' income. Remember, your corporation might consist of only you and your spouse, (making your spouse your only employee) and that money is completely tax-free until it is withdrawn in retirement. Of course, the contribution, as well as the money that the investment earns, will be taxed when it is withdrawn (except in the case of Roth IRAs—see below). The advantage is an immediate and substantial decrease in your tax liability. Moreover, this will doubly work to your advantage because you will most likely be in a lower tax bracket when you do retire. So, if everything works out right, the money will be taxed at a lower rate anyway!

With individual retirement strategy, there are a variety of plans which you can set up for your corporation, and you'd be wise to talk with a financial planner about which one best fits your companies' needs. There are some key factors to keep in mind, however, as you consider these different retirement plans. For example, qualified-pension or profit-sharing plans which include the 401(k) plans are used by C Corporations whereas SEP (Simplified

Employee Pension) or Keogh plans are used by sole proprietors. This is another example of the way the tax advantages the tax code offers to business people are more attractive than those offered to individuals.

Also keep in mind that in most cases, all of your employees must be provided equal opportunity to whichever plan you decide on. *Remember:* usually the money you contribute to these plans is going to be there for the long haul. Should you decide you need the money before you can legally start drawing from it at age 59 1/2, you'll end up paying huge penalties.

## Diversifying Your Corporation

I mentioned earlier that the image many people have of a C Corporation is usually inaccurate, and that many corporations are in fact just one person, a husband and wife, or one person and a couple of employees (who might even be your children). Another thing that might surprise you about corporations is that, sometimes, one person owns multiple corporations. So, for example, a person who owns a corporation that makes fish tanks might have another, completely separate, corporation that sells and distributes those fish tanks.

Why do people do this? One key reason is because different *types* of C Corporations and different *combinations* of C Corporations can benefit each other tremendously in terms of reducing your tax liability. Let's get a basic overview of how this works; then if you want to initiate any of these programs, you will know where to start. Of course, you're going to have to utilize the services of a tax professional to get something up and running (to ensure compliance with all federal, state, and local regulations and restrictions, etc.), but at least you will have a map to guide you.

Let's start with some examples of different types of relationships between corporations. First, you could have one corporation that owns stock in another (or more than one) corporation. That's known as a parent-subsidiary relationship. Or you might personally own the entire stock in two different corporations. In this case the relationship is called a brother-sister arrangement. There are different advantages to each of these relationships. For example, if you set up a subsidiary corporation that's owned by another corporation, which you also own, and if one of the two corporations shows a profit and the other shows a loss, then you could file a consolidated tax return so that the profits of one corporation would offset the losses in the other. If the losses in the one corporation equaled the profits of the other, you would have absolutely no tax liability because the net profit— the combination of the two profits from the two corporations—amounts to zero. This is a tactic that is used by many international corporations to reduce their tax liability.

Another strategy to consider is to make transactions between your two corporations. You might have one business that is in manufacturing, while the second corporation actually purchases product from the manufacturing corporation for distribution. The situation of a corporation that made fish tanks is an appropriate example (see above). This is an especially attractive option if one of your corporations is subject to large government restrictions—EPA considerations, for example—and your other business is not. This is because, typically, marketing corporations are not subject to as many governmental restrictions as are manufacturers.

Oftentimes different types of corporations are also subject to different types and different degrees of taxes. This is especially true when you consider that different states have different tax rates. It's very possible that you could lower your combined tax liability by establishing a transaction that moves money from one corporation to another, even from one state to another. For instance, suppose you've got a very successful business in New York State where the taxes are very high. To help ease this burden, at least partially, you could actually set up a second C corporation in Nevada that no one in New York even knows exists. The Nevada corporation, then, could charge management fees to the New York corporation, and in so doing, you'd be transferring money from 'high-tax' New York to 'low-tax' Nevada, effectively lowering your corporations' combined tax liability. Still confused? Let's consider another way to utilize the same strategy.

Most of us have, at one time or another, hired consultants or management companies to work with or for us. Along the same lines, you could have a Nevada-based management company that consults with your New York-based business. For example, let's say you own an apartment complex in New York. You probably need help managing it, or at least consultation. There's no reason why the consulting company you use couldn't be based in Nevada, nor is there any reason why you can't also own the consulting company. This way, you also have less liability tied into your New York corporation, meaning there's less likelihood anyone will want to spend much money or effort attacking you legally.

I have clients who own a giant construction firm. They have their equipment in one corporation, they do their business in another, and all their employees work for a leasing company. That makes three corporations. Leaving the tax benefits aside, if one of the corporations were ever to be sued, their total assets would never be in jeopardy and none of the corporations could be sued to compensate for the lack of assets in another.

*Note:* The number of companies you own is very much dependent on their value. If you have a net worth of, say, $25,000, you don't want to set up 14 different corporations to protect yourself. However, you might, if your company is worth $300,000.

## Corporations as Property Owners

Sometimes there are benefits to taking some of the real estate property you own personally and transferring it into a C Corporation. This will not always work to your advantage, however, so read this section carefully—you might be better off maintaining personal ownership of the property.

There are two main reasons why you would want to put property into your corporation. First, you may own property that you don't want anyone to *know* you own. For example, if you have property in Iowa that you want to keep safe from creditors, you could put it into a corporation that you own in Nevada. This way, since there are no records indicating that you *personally* own the property, there is virtually no way for a creditor to link you to this property. In fact, in Nevada, you don't even have to list yourself as a corporate officer. You can list an officer nominee, or designee, and your name wouldn't even appear in the Nevada County Register where the corporation is listed. In this case, the property "owner" would appear as the corporation's name, allowing you to maintain your privacy and protect your assets. And take it from me, when it comes to running a business, the better you are able to protect your assets, the better off you will be in general. The following will illustrate this point:

I know a man who owned a house in southern California worth several hundred thousand dollars. He came to the National Audit Defense Network; one of our agents advised him take out a mortgage in the name of a corporation he owned in Nevada. This way, if he ever got sued, lawyers wouldn't think he had any assets in southern California. Shortly thereafter, while he was on vacation, his son was arrested for selling narcotics. He was very upset, of course, but breathed a sigh of relief when one of the arresting officers told him that if he hadn't had a 95% mortgage on his house they could have seized it under RICO (Racketeer Influenced and Corrupt Organization Act) statutes for violating drug laws. Naturally, he would have ultimately recovered his house since he wasn't involved in the drug sales. But imagine the grief, as well as the legal expenses, of having to repossess your wrongly-seized house. It was only because the house was legally owned by a separate Nevada corporation that the police never found out the house actually belonged to him.

Thus, I would strongly encourage those of you who have substantial assets to explore this as an option to lower your tax liability, because in our litigious society there seems to be the risk of a lawsuit at every turn. An attorney will agree that you should do everything you can to protect your personal assets in order to lower the chance that someone's will separate you from everything you've worked so hard for all your life.

If you have a corporation that happens to be doing a lot of business and accumulating a lot of assets, it would probably be to your advantage to transfer out any property that your *corporation* owns for the same reason.  So this way, if someone sues the company, there will be less *company* assets at risk, leaving you protected once again.

## Gifts to Your Children

In addition to the estate-tax advantages of giving money and shares of your company to your children, there are other advantages in giving gifts that will immediately reduce your tax liability even as your company is growing.  You can give outright gifts of up to $10,000 in cash or income-producing property, per person, to your children or anyone else, for example.  If you and your spouse give the gifts jointly, you can give up to $20,000 per person per year.  All of this money is tax-free; no gift-tax return is required of the donor, as long as the gift does not exceed these limits.

*Note:* although it is legal and can sometimes be prudent to give these types of gifts to minors, in most cases it isn't a good strategy.  You're better off transferring money to the accounts of your children who are mature enough in the eyes of the IRS to manage their own finances and these gifts.  Also keep in mind that the money or property must truly be gifts, and cannot, for example, be in lieu of court-ordered financial support.

# Hiring Spouses and Other Family Members

Employing family members is sort of like playing poker with friends. That is, you *could* go to Las Vegas, or Reno, or Atlantic City and buy into a poker game with a group of strangers. For example, perhaps you've bought into a game of seven-card stud, and you've got aces and eights—not great cards, but good enough that you stay in until the call. Unfortunately you might lose, maybe to three kings, and after the house takes its cut, the guy across the table gets your money. And unless you get lucky, you'll never see him, or your money, again.

On the other hand, you could play with friends. A colleague of mine likes to go to the Vegas tables with four or five friends, and they all buy in together thereby greatly increasing the chances that the money they bring into the casino collectively will leave with their group. Even after the house takes its cut, it's a lot easier to see that an $80 pot went to your friend at the office, or your softball teammate than to a complete stranger. After all, there's at least a halfway decent chance he'll buy you a drink with the money on the way out.

For the same reasons, it's good to hire family members because it increases the amount of money that will stay in the family. That is, as profits are made, rather than redistributing this money to unassociated employees, you can pay it to people in your own family. Don't forget, of course, that the family member must do legitimate work. You can't simply have a family member on your payroll, who never actually comes into the office. In the event that you are audited, you *must* be able to demonstrate that every person on your payroll did, in fact, work to maintain or further the profit objective of your business. Again, good record-keeping is essential. I suggest not only making entries in your daily log, but also keeping accurate time sheets for the work performed by your employees/family members. It's also a good idea to pay by check, and to keep the canceled checks on file.

Another thing to keep in mind is that the compensation the employee receives must be reasonable. That is, you cannot pay a 12-year-old child $75 an hour to sharpen pencils, dust your desk, and run to the post office. You could pay her minimum wage, however, even if she's too young to otherwise be employed at a minimum-wage job. Generally speaking, a child becomes eligible for employment in your company at age seven, at which time she's eligible to receive at least minimum-wage pay for bona fide work.

It's also critical to understand the difference between sole proprietorships hiring family members and corporations hiring family members. If you are a sole proprietor, you can legally hire your under-eighteen-year-old children and pay them without taking deductions for Social Security. On the other hand, as a corporation, you absolutely must pay those taxes. Hiring your children can also be advantageous because even if they don't earn the maximum allowable by the IRS ($4,550 per child, or $7,550 if you set up a $3,000 IRA), they're still getting real work experience. If you take the time to walk your children through the whole process of getting a job, like posting an ad, having them apply, interviewing them, and having them sign their time sheets, they will have gained an invaluable knowledge about the way real business operates. Moreover, this process will only help you add to the paper trail (via their resumes, letters of application, etc.) that you will keep for your tax records. Meanwhile, they can spend the money they earn. You could even invest it in a savings account for college.

Finally, the Internal Revenue Service allows you to set up tax-deductible medical benefit plans in your employee or family member's names (see Chapter 8). In certain cases, this can mean taking out a policy for your spouse that covers *her* spouse—you! The only consideration is that you must offer the same benefits to all of your full-time employees.

# Charitable Contributions

Let's say your business had a good year. Your numbers were up; life is good. You look around and see that not everyone else in the world is in the same boat. Organizations need money for research, universities need money to update their technology, and thousands of families every year are in need of money just to feed and clothe their children. Thankfully, you can help out, and dramatically reduce your tax liability at the same time. Simply by giving money, inventory, stock, or even old materials and equipment your business no longer needs, you can do something for the good of others and, at the same time, pay less in taxes. For example, suppose your corporation is getting toward the end of its fiscal year and you have a lot of cash, which will surely be taxed unless you find some way to spend it. A far better option than paying out the excess in dividends is to turn that money into a charitable donation. In fact, as an individual, you can donate up to 50% of your income to a legitimate charity or up to 30% of appreciated capital-gain property, and simultaneously decrease those important end-of-the-year figures that determine how much tax you pay.

Corporations are limited to a deduction of 10% of taxible

income under current law. This is another advantage of the C Corporation which isn't available to sole proprietorships, although it is to individual taxpayers.

Individual taxpayers can take charitable donations and write them off as personal expenses if they itemize. This is a good thing to know, even if you can't afford to make huge cash donations to Easter Seals, the American Cancer Society, and other worthwhile causes which qualify. The key is simply to keep receipts of your material donations. For example, if your garage is overflowing with things you don't want or need, you *could* have a yard sale. You could spend days putting up flyers, pricing your old bent flatware, ripped lawn chairs, strollers, skis, toaster ovens, etc., and then get up really early one Saturday morning to spend a day haggling pennies with garage-sale hunter. When you're all done, you might go the bank and deposit the $37 you made and take what didn't sell to the Salvation Army drop-off site. On the other hand, you could figure out what it's all worth, put it into a big pile in your garage and call the Salvation Army to come pick it up.  Remember, most of these types of organizations provide receipts but let *you* fill in the value amount. Of course, you must be reasonable in how you fill out the receipt, but that old lamp that wouldn't fetch $5 at your yard sale might legitimately be worth $30, $50, or more as a deduction. So, you have your choice: $5 cash in your hand or a $50 write-off.

Getting back to corporations, many people privately give substantial amounts of money each year to their favorite charities like churches, research organizations, museums, or symphonies. I admire this, but the truth is, there are certain strategies available by using your C Corporation to make these same donations that will benefit you more.  Normally, when you make a charitable contribution in cash you pay your tax first. You see what's left of your income after taxes and then try to take out enough to make a little charitable contribution. Oftentimes, that means after you pay, say, 50% of your income to the government, you're looking to scrape together a donation. With a business, you can make the contribution first. Let's say I get paid $100 for a consulting job I did, and I want to give that money to charity. I've got to pay taxes on it first—income tax, Social Security tax, Medicare tax, state and local taxes, etc. Well this might leave me with $60 to donate to my charity of choice, and $60 to write off on April 15th. However, if I wanted to, I could give money to that same charity before I pay the taxes, and give them the full $100. That way, everyone comes out ahead. The charity gets $40 more to spend, and I get to deduct $40 more from my end-of-the-year tax liability.

Keep in mind that the increase on any inventory that your corporation owns is subject to tax because the inventory is applied to your tax liability. However, if you were to donate that inventory—that is, the amount equal to the increase in value—to a charity, you wouldn't be responsible for paying taxes on its value.

In addition to donating money or inventory to charity, you can donate stock. Naturally, as the value of your company increases, so does the value of your stock. As stock value increases, so does your tax liability. If you sell the stock, you would be taxed on it. On the other hand, if you gave stock to a charitable organization, your corporation could deduct 100% of the contribution. The charity could now sell the stock and use the proceeds to fund beneficial programs. As a matter of fact, as your corporation grows, you can give away up to 49% of your stock, and still maintain control.

Finally, the Internal Revenue Service allows for the donation of real property, generally at its fair-market value. Like stock, gifts of property make the most sense when it has increased in value and there is a significant difference between its original value and its current value. The difference is an unrealized profit, or "paper profit," on which you are not taxed. Other forms of legitimate charitable donations include artistic work, company services, tickets purchased for fundraisers, memberships to museums, and life insurance policies. As I've said all along, the key is to keep good records, and in the case of property donations, reliable witnesses.

## To Whom Can I Donate?

In order for your donation or contribution to be tax deductible, the organization to which you donate must qualify in the eyes of the IRS. One way to find out for sure whether your intended recipient qualifies is to get the annually updated IRS Publication 78 from the Treasury Department. Available online at www.irs.gov, it lists the different types of qualified organizations and also provides donation limits. In general, organizations must be U.S.-based and not involved in any sort of political lobbying. Additionally, the organization's earnings must not benefit individuals. Examples of qualifying organizations are churches, publicly supported universities, medical/research organizations, and community trusts.

Keep in mind that there are certain strategies for targeting your donations that will make the donated dollars go farthest. For example, suppose you would like to contribute to the medical expenses of a Little League ballplayer who injured himself in a game and whose parents have no medical insurance (and, for the sake or argument, let's assume the league has no insurance of its own).

Instead of giving the money directly to the parents, who are not recognized as a legitimate charity in the eyes of the IRS, you could give the money to the tax-exempt Little League organization and receive a 100% donation. Technically, the league can choose how to spend that money, but the understanding, of course, is that it will be spent to cover the medical expenses of the injured player.

# Adjusting Salaries

One of the most interesting and useful advantages of operating your business as a C Corporation is that it allows you to raise or adjust your own salary depending on your particular needs. As odd as it might first seem, as a general rule you don't want to take a big salary from your corporation. If you do, you will end up paying more than you needed to pay in income tax, as well as Social Security, Medicare, and other taxes. In some cases, you might *want* to temporarily increase your salary. You may, for example, want to buy a new home, and even though your corporation might be worth a lot of money, the corporation is a separate entity that does not reflect your *personal* credit history. And because you need a personal loan in order to finance your new home, a year or two before you actually apply for the loan, you simply give yourself a little raise. The goal is to lift your salary to a point that will look good on paper. Then once you've qualified for your loan and bought the home, you rework a salary reduction. This way, you once again reduce your own personal tax liability and transfer a good portion of the capital back to your corporation, which, as you know by now, affords far more possibilities for tax-liability reduction than what is available to an individual.

Let's take this a step further. Say you decide to raise your salary in order to qualify for the house loan, but this raise actually puts your C Corporation into a position where your corporation shows a net loss. You can now take this loss and apply it to one of the two previously profitable years and actually reduce your tax liability for one or both of those years. In some cases, this could actually mean a small refund coming your way!

# Interest Deductions

It should go without saying that the more you know and understand about our system of taxation, the better prepared you'll be to legally lower your tax liability. Of course, understanding our overly complicated Tax Code is no simple matter, and the Internal Revenue Service relies to some degree on our being intimidated by the language and length of the tax code. Because so many of us are intimidated, we end up paying far more in taxes than our fair share.

One area that gets particularly difficult—but an area that taxpayers should have at least a basic familiarity—is that of interest. Obviously, there are many different kinds of interest, created from many more different types of business endeavors. The more you know about how the Internal Revenue Service views interest, the better position you'll be in come April 15th. Generally, personal interest cannot be claimed as a tax deduction. This includes interest on personal loans, credit cards, etc., excepting interest on mortgages and student loans. This even includes interest on taxes *owed* to the IRS; an individual cannot write off interest from tax deficiencies.

Businesses can, however, write off interest owed to the IRS. That is, interest that has been imposed by the IRS for tax deficiencies attributable to your business can be used as a business deduction. This is one more reason you should put forth every effort to convert your hobbies and personal interests into some type of home business.

# Trust Funds

Another interesting area of taxation, that does not strictly lead to money-saving strategies but must be reviewed for your protection, is the tax-withholding trust fund. Indeed, mistakes in the handling of a tax-withholding trust fund can lead to some of the saddest IRS abuse stories I've heard.

As you know, if you have a business, you must set aside money to pay income tax, Social Security, Medicare, etc., and this money goes into a trust fund that's being paid to the government. If, for any reason, you don't pay into that trust fund, the IRS will surely come looking for you. Forgetting to pay into this fund is considered a major "no-no" by the IRS. In fact, the government will not only make sure that you get caught up on your trust fund account, but it will also levy disproportionate fines by way of penalties, and often times even prosecute offenders.

These penalties can often be levied unfairly because it is sometimes the case that the person who ends up taking the blame when the contribution isn't made is not actually the one responsible for making the contribution. For example, you're a bookkeeper or secretary and have absolutely no say in the day-to-day workings of the company for which you work, except that you are allowed to be a signer on the company accounts. Now, let's say your boss goes out of town on business or vacation, and you, who have been granted only the most limited amount of authority, have to sign some checks for the company. Usually, this will not cause a problem, but suppose the company goes belly-up and there are unpaid trust funds. Now, because you signed checks, you could be held responsible. Imagine, one day you're a secretary making $9 an hour, and the next you're liable for $200,000 in payroll taxes, plus interest and penalties—all because your boss closed the business and is nowhere to be found.

My story is hypothetical, but I know people who have been literally forced into bankruptcy and had their lives ruined by situations like this. So a word of warning: if you're not in a position of control, be very careful before signing on accounts where trust funds are distributed, because the IRS may come after you, and require you to pay those trust fund monies *even if* they know you had nothing to do with it. In fact, they can pursue controllers, bookkeepers, secretaries, corporate officers, presidents, and CEOs.

Of course, the Internal Revenue Service cannot make one individual liable for the taxes of another individual or entity. That is, if a corporation such as General Motors doesn't pay its payroll taxes, the IRS can't come after me, Robert Bennington. But like everything else, the IRS has ways around this little problem. They call it a penalty. Instead of making me liable for those taxes, they can say, "Hey, Mr. Bennington, we're going to penalize you for *your role* in the company's delinquent payroll taxes." Guess what? The amount of the penalty is exactly the same amount as the taxes that weren't paid. That's right, its 100%!

So, the moral of the story is, if you have an S corporation, C corporation, or limited liability business that doesn't pay its payroll taxes, you personally can be held liable. To avoid that situation, make sure that if your company gets into financial trouble, the first thing you pay off is the trust fund tax, even if it's at the expense of other creditors. Remember, these other creditors can't penalize you *personally* like the IRS can. In addition, when you write the check to the IRS, make sure you clearly indicate *on the check* that the money can only be applied against the trust fund portion of the liability. Instructing that the check cannot be used for other income taxes is crucial because a nice little trick the IRS will use is to arbitrarily assign money intended for trust funds to other taxes owed—then they come after you personally because you haven't taken care of the trust fund liability. They will include the 100% penalty to boot!

## Independent Contractors

It's becoming frequently common for companies to hire independent contractors to perform certain services for the business. Basically, an independent contractor is defined as someone who has been hired to do a job, but can't be told exactly when or how to do it. A university might, for example, hire someone to come in and administer a test, or a large company might hire someone to hold a special seminar on personnel management. Generally, if you're an independent contractor, you are being hired as though you were a separate company, mainly because the employer is not responsible for withholding Social Security or income tax for you. For this and other reasons, the Internal Revenue Service has been cracking down on independent contractors, and likewise, more and more independent contractors are coming to NADN with big IRS problems.

If the IRS determines that you should have been an employee instead of an independent contractor, you will not be allowed to use your Schedule C to report all your income and expenses. Instead, all of your income will be reported as earned wages and all of your expenses as itemized deductions. Therefore, you will lose some of the tax benefits of those deductions, if that. One key difference will be an increase in the Social Security tax you pay if you are an independent contractor, and you might even be subject to the alternative minimum tax added on top of the amount you owe.

The corporation that employed you was owned by you; therefore, the same rules may also apply. If you have a C corporation, dividend payment is even worse because no deduction is allowed to the corporation as a business expense, and you have to pay income tax on the dividend.

In short, my advice to independent contractors is to be aware that, if you decide to declare this as your occupation, the IRS will surely be watching you. Like I always say, get professional tax help. The small investment in a professional tax service will provide many happy returns.

## The Disguised-Dividend Trap

I hope I've made it clear that dividends are generally a poor way for your company to pay you because they're not deductible to the business. Dividends are defined as distributions of the earnings and profits of a corporation. It is important to remember that these earnings and profits have already been taxed once to the corporation itself, assuming it is a C Corporation. It is also important to remember that these dividends are taxable again upon distribution to you.

Many times, owners of incorporated small businesses find they have inadvertently paid dividends to themselves. For example, let's say a corporation paid some personal expenses for you, a shareholder, perhaps as a result of travel expenses, entertainment, or gifts. Now, it's quite possible that the Internal Revenue Service will claim the expenses were not legitimate. In that case, the IRS will likely call these reimbursements "dividend distributions" to you. Again, you're going to be much better off in such a case if you've kept meticulous records and can document your expenses. As always, you want to maintain a strong cache of ammunition should you be audited. Even if you lose at the audit, you'll still be able to bring plenty of documentation to the IRS appeal process.

## The Passive-Loss Trap

Another area of potential danger is the passive-loss trap. Passive investments, as defined and identified by the Internal Revenue Code, are business investments in which you don't take part in the daily operational management. Real estate is a good example. Suppose, for example, that you own an apartment complex across town. If your income is less than $150,000 and you're active in managing the property, then you can write off a loss of up to $25,000 to offset non-passive income.

This is an area that ultimately gets quite complicated and a full discussion is beyond the scope of this book. My advice is to be aware of income that you might be incurring passively and to talk to your tax planner about the possibilities and pitfalls of passive losses. This way, you're less likely to be caught off guard at the end of the year.

# Loan Repayments

The Internal Revenue Service also looks very closely at the repayment of money loaned, advanced, or invested by shareholders. Unless this money qualifies as repayment of a bona fide loan, these payments could be considered by the IRS as dividend distribution. For example, if your company loans you $20,000, you have every intention of paying it back. You need to be cautious because the IRS always scrutinizes such loans closely. The first step is to ensure that you've got a clear loan repayment agreement—so you must be very careful with the way it's worded. If you don't have an agreement that will hold up to IRS and judicial scrutiny, the government could conceivably claim that you are merely scheming a way for your company to give you the money as a dividend distribution. As always, leave a clear and professional paper trail.

# Mum's The Word

Remember that your C Corporation is a legally separate entity, even if it is owned by you as an individual. In the case of the new-home loan above, if you (as the owner of a C Corporation) wanted to disclose both your individual and corporation financial records, you could. On the other hand, you are under absolutely no legal obligation to show the lending institution, for instance, your corporate tax returns when you apply for a personal loan. You also do not have to disclose your ownership of a C corporation on your individual tax returns; although, in justifying your salary, you would indicate that you're an officer of the company. In fact, you could set up an operation in which you don't draw a salary at all, and in this case, there would be no reason why anyone would ever know you were involved with the corporation.

Why would you want to do this? The answer is simple— privacy. The fewer people who know you have a C Corporation, the fewer people there are to come after you and your assets in a lawsuit. The truth is, if someone wants to sue you, the first thing a lawyer will do is run what's called an "asset search" to find out exactly what, and how much, you own. If you owned a C Corporation in Nevada, however, where you do not have to legally declare your ownership, an asset search would reveal only your personal assets. In other words, it would appear as if you owned far less than you actually did.

Remember, lawyers usually don't care what the judgment is, they only care about what they can get their hands on. If the judgment against you is $1.5 million dollars and your personal assets total $35,000, then even if you've got $6 million in a properly structured corporation, these assets are not only off limits, but no one even knows about the extra assets. Therefore, anyone considering a lawsuit against you would likely decide it's not worth the effort; they may try to find someone whose assets are within reach.

# Chapter Eleven

# Retirement Strategies

*"Knowledge itself is power."*
**-Francis Bacon, *Religious Meditations***

*"Would twenty shillings have ruined Mr. Hampden's fortune?*
*No! but the payment of half twenty shillings, on the principle*
*it was demanded, would have made him a slave."*
**-Edmund Burke,**
**"Speech on American Taxation" (1774)**

Although more Americans than ever are starting to realize the real need for private retirement plans, most people still only think about retirement one dimensionally. That is, they only think about retirement as "the money I will need to live on when I'm old." This is only half of the benefit. Retirement plans provide a dynamic opportunity for you to enjoy immediate tax breaks. When used strategically, retirement planning is a cornerstone of good tax planning.

There are a variety of retirement plans to which you can contribute. The one you choose will depend greatly on your age, your income, the size of your company, and how much you want or can afford to contribute. To help you navigate this critical area, we will review several of the most popular private retirement plans. Keep in mind that some of these plans may only be available once you start your own business. Also, note that none of these plans are mutually exclusive. That is, just because you choose to fund one doesn't mean that you can't fund others as well. In fact, sometimes its advantageous to have two or more plans working simultaneously.

There are two basic types of retirement programs to which you can contribute: those designed for employees and those designed for the self-employed. Generally, plans designed for the self-employed allow for the greatest tax deferral. Changes made to plan rules as a result of the Economic Growth and Tax Relief Reconciliation Act of 2001 (EGTRA) allow for even greater flexibility in using retirement plans as an effective tax reduction strategy. Let's first look at plans designed for self-employed persons.

# Defined Contribution Plans

### *Profit Sharing*

The main advantage of the profit-sharing plan is flexibility. This is particularly so because it allows you to vary the amount of your annual contribution. This is a great advantage for businesses whose incomes aren't predictable thus making their profits variable. With this plan, while you might contribute the maximum allowable amount of the lesser of $25,000 or 13.0435% of your net income one year, you might choose the following year to contribute absolutely nothing.

The profit-sharing plan can be ideal for certain types of sole proprietors or partnerships. For example, let's say you're a travel writer and make all your income from royalties. Each time a new edition of your book comes out, it's in the front of the publisher's catalogue and generally aggressively marketed. On top of that, distributors and bookstores have been eagerly awaiting your book. The publisher prints 10,000 copies, and 6,500 copies are sold the first month. Now if the book retails for $20 and your royalty rate is 15%, then your royalty for that first month is $19,500. However, once all of the wholesalers have made their purchases and the book has been distributed to bookstores around the country, sales are going to slow down. In fact, let's suppose the remaining 3,500 copies of the first print run take the rest of the year to sell and the follow-up print run is 2,000 copies. You sell these in the second year and then get to work on your new edition. But for now you've earned $36,000 on the book: $30,000 the first year, $6,000 the second. With the profit-sharing plan, in the first year—when you're in a higher tax bracket—you sock away the maximum allowance into your retirement plan thus decreasing your taxable income by $3,913.50; the following year you don't contribute a penny.

Additionally, although you must offer the profit-sharing plan to your employees, the Internal Revenue Service allows a three-year grace period between the time you hire your employees and the time they become vested in the plan.

### Money Purchase

The money-purchase plan offers one of the highest contribution limits of all qualified retirement plans. In fact, you can contribute the lesser of $35,000 or 20% of net income. Unlike the profit-sharing plan, the money-purchase plan is a better fit for businesses with incomes that don't fluctuate much from year to year. Unlike the profit-sharing plan, however, the money-purchase plan requires that once you have established the amount of your annual contribution, you must contribute that same amount every year. So, if you start this kind of plan, you must be confident that you will be able to contribute that same amount each year until you retire.

### *Combination Plan*

As the name implies, the combination plan is a mix of contributions to both a money-purchase and a profit-sharing plan. In essence you split your contribution between the two plans so that in years where your income may vary, you can gain some flexibility in your plan contribution amount. You are still required to contribute the fixed amount to the money-purchase plan, but you can alter your contribution to the profit-sharing plan.

## Defined Benefit Plan

Defined benefit plans have a decidedly more narrow appeal than those I've discussed so far, but in some cases they're ideal. This plan is best suited for well-established companies with senior, well-compensated employees who are within ten or fifteen years of retirement. Defined Benefit Plans allow for the greatest contribution level of all self-employed plans. You can contribute the lesser of $140,000 or 100% of average net income during the three highest earning years. There is another distinction—they work backwards. In other words, instead of deciding how much you can afford to contribute per month, or what percentage of your income you want deposited in the package, you decide how much you want the plan to be worth when you retire. So you first decide how much money you will need each month to live the kind of lifestyle you desire, and then you figure out exactly how to get there and what your contributions to the plan need to be.

So why doesn't this appeal to everyone? The answer is that while this type of plan does allow for larger contributions, it's also extremely expensive to administer, in large part because it requires the assistance of an actuary. Depending on where you live, actuary services could run as high as $10,000.

# SEP IRAs [408(k)]

At the other end of the cost spectrum is the SEP (self employed) individual retirement account (IRA). This is the simplest of all plans and anyone with self-employment income can contribute to this plan. You can contribute 13.0435% of your self-employment income up to a maximum of $25,000, to this IRA. The plan has no reporting requirements and can be set-up by most banks and brokerage firms including the leading on-line firms. The plan does not require an annual contribution, and unlike the other plans discussed so far, you can make a contribution to the plan up to the due date for filing your tax return (generally April 15th of the following year). By allowing for a later contribution date, you can still enjoy the holiday season and contribute to your IRA after you have paid for all of your holiday purchases.

Now, before you despair that there are no options for wage earners, believe me, there are some great plans for you. Let's take a look.

# Individual Retirement Accounts

### *Traditional IRAs*

Anyone under age 70 with earned income can contribute to an IRA. For 2002, you can contribute up to $3000 to an IRA. As long as you are not an active participant in an employer-sponsored plan, your contribution is fully deductible from your gross income. You can make the contribution at anytime during the year and up until the original filing deadline for your tax return. And there is good news for those of your reading this book who are over 50 years of age! Beginning in 2002, you can contribute an additional $500 to your IRA in order to "catch up" your contributions.

### *Spousal IRAs*

If you are married and only one spouse has earned income, you can still benefit from an IRA. The spousal IRA allows a non-working spouse to contribute to their own IRA based on their spouse's earned income. Just like the traditional IRA, the non-working spouse can contribute $3000 ($3500 if they are 50 years of age or older) to the IRA and claim the deduction on their joint return. This deduction is even available to the non-working spouse if their spouse is contributing to an employer–sponsored plan. The only problem is the deduction phases out in this case when their adjusted gross income is between $150,000 - $160,000. Imagine, that could mean a reduction of your taxable income by $7000.

### *Roth IRAs*

The Roth IRA was introduced with the Taxpayer Relief Act of 1997 and is different from all other IRAs in one major respect: the contributions you make are not deductible, but in return you are not taxed later on the earnings in the account. For example, you still pay taxes on a $1000 contribution you make in a calendar year, but twenty years down the road, when you're withdrawing $1500 a month as your retirement, that money will be completely tax free. In fact, you do not even need to wait twenty years to start withdrawing from a Roth IRA. As long as the account is at least five years old and you are 59 1/2 , you can make tax-free withdrawals from the account. Also, if you plan to purchase your first home, you can take a tax free distribution from your Roth IRA to help pay for your house as long as the account is older than five years.

### *Education IRA – Coverdell Education Savings Account*

The Coverdell Education Savings Account (ESA), formerly known as an Education IRA, is a trust established to pay qualified education expenses of a designated beneficiary. While you might not think of this as a retirement plan, the ESA is included in this chapter because it works much like a Roth IRA. That is, the contributions are not tax deductible, however, the earnings are tax deferred and distributions are tax free if used to pay qualified education expenses of the beneficiary.

One of the great things about the ESA is that the beneficiary does not have to be your child. Any child under age 18 can have an ESA and accept contributions into the account up to an annual maximum of $2000. That way, aunts, uncles, grandparents, family, and/or friends can make a contribution to the educational needs of the child.

The ESA has undergone sweeping changes since it was first introduced in 1997. Beginning in 2002, qualified educational expenses have been expanded to include elementary and secondary education expenses as well as higher education expenses. These expenses now include tuition, fees, books, supplies, equipment, academic tutoring, the purchase of computer technology or equipment or Internet access, and expenses for room and board, uniforms, and transportation. While the AGI phase out for contributors still exists, that person could gift the $2000 to the beneficiary and then have the child put that money into the ESA.

In my opinion, if you have kids, then an ESA is one of the most attractive tax strategies available to you. There is no limit on the number of accounts you can set up and fund, nor does your funding an ESA have any bearing on any other retirement plan. In fact, you might find that it compliments your profit sharing, Roth IRA, or other retirement plan. Remember, a corporation can also make a contribution to the account. Another benefit of the ESA is that the funds can be rolled over into another ESA for different family members. Let's say your daughter decides not to pursue any formal education beyond next year, but your son is going to head for the ivy leagues. You can roll over the money from your daughter's ESA into your son's ESA and still gain all of the advantages of the tax-deferred growth.

# Chapter Twelve

# Gift and Estate Taxes

*"Yet take these gifts, brought as our fathers bade,*
*For sorrow's tribute to the passing shade."*
**-Catallus, A Book of Airs,**
**(tr. by Sir William Marris)**

*"Have you built your ship of death, O have you?*
*O build your ship of death, for you will need it."*
**-D. H Lawrence, "The Ship of Death"**

---

## Disclaimer

As this edition went to press, Congress had passed sweeping changes to the estate and gift tax laws. Due to the complexities of these changes and some additional pending changes contained in the proposed economic stimulus legislation, the contents of this chapter apply to laws in effect during 2001 and would be valid for completing tax forms for that year. For updated information concerning estate and gift tax laws, please contact a tax specialist at NADN or visit our website at www.awayirs.com.

By now you no doubt realize that I harbor deep misgivings about the amount and types of taxes we, as citizens of the United States, pay each April 15. We pay income tax, sales tax, property tax, Social Security, Medicare, and so on and so forth. In fact, many times Americans don't realize just how much they pay in taxes to Uncle Sam, or where this money goes.

That said, however, I personally feel that of all these taxes, the most insidious and harmful to society, are federal estate and gift taxes. Consider the life we lead as adult members of this country. We make a little money, buy a car, a small home, maybe even start a business, all the while crossing our fingers that we'll make it to the end of each month and still have enough money to take our family out to dinner and the movies. We ask ourselves time and time again, "Where does the money go? We haven't even bought that much stuff." That's right, we haven't. Moreover, the money we use to purchase these assets is money on which we pay taxes. We continue through the years and slowly build up an estate. We find we're actually worth something, even if we are still scrambling at the end of the month. Sooner or later, we die. We are, as Horace wrote over 2,000 years ago, "but dust and a shadow." When our heirs try to assume position of our estate, however, everything is mysteriously taxed all over again. Uncle Sam steps in, holds out his greedy hands, and levies the infamous "death tax" on assets we paid taxes on all our lives.

I'm not alone in thinking that this is unfair and needs to be addressed by our federal government. In fact, in the summer of 2000, both the United States Congress and Senate voted to repeal the "death tax," under the belief that it was doing far more harm than good. Unfortunately, President Clinton vetoed this bill effectively denied thousands of legitimate heirs the rights to their families' hard-earned money. Gift taxes create essentially the same problem. You work hard. You stash a little money away. But when you decide you want to give someone some of this money as a gift, you're forced to pay taxes on the gift, even though you've *already* paid taxes on the money when you earned it.

Changes to these unfair forms of "double taxation" are among the many things we at the National Audit Defense Network lobby for every year. In the meantime, however, until the law is changed and estate and gift taxes are repealed, there are some strategies you can take advantage of to reduce these double taxes.

Many of you probably think that federal estate tax laws only hurt the truly rich, owners of companies big companies like Microsoft and Nike. To a degree, you're right. The bigger a company is or the bigger the potential gift or estate becomes, the higher the individual tax becomes. In fact, estate taxes can be as high as 60% of the total value of an estate!

Think about your own estate and the assets you have collected over the course of your lifetime. The home you bought when you were first starting out might have appreciated considerably. For example, over 20 years' time a home can appreciate as much as 400%, perhaps more. Who knows? With the way the stock market's been climbing these last several years those stocks you bought fifteen years ago and put in a drawer suddenly might be worth a good deal of money. Perhaps you even own a little rental property that you bought one year when your profits were high. You see, assets add up quickly. But just *try* to pass these assets on to your children. You could be subjected to taxes at the very same rate the big companies are: 60%. Think about this for a moment. You pay, say 40% federal income tax, 8-10% state taxes, and then another 60% in estate taxes! Obviously, this is a huge problem.  In fact, I recently read that 90% of all family-owned businesses don't survive to the third generation. Why?  Because when families go to pay the federal estate tax, the only way they can afford to do so, is to "sell the farm," so to speak. I believe  this defeats the purpose of a family business and goes against the very grain of what this country stands for.  If a family builds a successful business, *that* family ought to be able to pass it on to future generations without costly and punitive estate taxes.

If you do end up selling your house as you pass on your estate, don't make the mistake of many people and assume that the amount you put down for your house is your basis.  Your basis is the total cost of the house.  The amount of your mortgage doesn't matter. Also keep in mind that "what you paid for the house" can include what you paid for improvements.  For example, if you added a porch, a bedroom or bathroom, or even a second story, this all increases your home's basis.  Homeowners in the past have argued their cases in front of the IRS, and have sometimes done very well.  As is always the case, those who have kept the best records have done the best. If your general contractor did the work, keep his final bill; if you did it yourself, keep receipts from every nail, screw, piece of lumber, bucket of paint, light-switch plate, and jar of spackling compound.  Also, be sure to keep copies of all permits required by local ordinances. Then put all these records away somewhere safe. You might not need them for 10, 15, even 20 years, but someday, when you go pass your property to your children, you'll be glad you were able to prove your home's true basis.

Basis is also important for income-tax purposes when you give someone a gift. Let's say, for example, you decide to give your house to your children. The government is going to carry over the $100,000 that you originally paid for the home (this is the basis). So if the home is now worth twice that amount, the IRS is going to look at the original cost as the basis your children would use to calculate any future capital gain.

The other important consideration for estate tax and gift tax evaluations is the fair market value of the estate or gift. The fair market value is defined as what someone would pay for the asset if she were to buy it today. So is the same house that you paid $100,000 ten years ago now worth $200,000? How do you know? That is determined by appraisals. Are other homes in the neighborhood selling for the same amount? If they are and they have roughly the same square footage, are in about the same condition, and their landscaping is similar, then the fair market value is $200,000, while the basis remains $100,000.

Obviously, fair market value can be very difficult to determine. Is the home on the corner worth more, or less, than the one next door? Exactly how much value was added by upgrading you home to dual-pane windows? What's that swimming pool worth? For these reasons, professional appraisers— the same folks who appraise property for lending institutions—are often used. In fact, it's very likely that the Internal Revenue Service will require you to obtain the services of a professional appraiser to determine your property's fair market value.

In some cases, there are less complicated ways to determine an asset's value. For example, in the case of automobiles, a price quoted by Kelly Blue Book is going to be completely acceptable. You can obtain a free quote from Kelly by visiting their web site at www.kbb.com.

Note that many of these same points apply to stocks as well. For example, if you give your children stock on January 1, 2002, it will have a definite value. You need to record the transfer of this stock because if the stock goes up in value, the IRS could hit you up for additional taxes by claiming that the stock is worth more now. Thus, you need to be able to demonstrate that you gave the stock to your children when it was worth $3,500, not after it soared to $12,000. *Remember:* you can give each of your children up to $10,000 a year in gifts without having to file a gift tax return—see Chapter 6.

# Your Will

The foundation for all estate planning is your will. The *structure* your will is of critical importance for several reasons: first, you want to make sure that your assets are not tied up in courts for years after your death. Second, you want to make sure everything goes as smoothly as possible for your loved ones during their time of grief (the last thing they need is nosy IRS agents complicating things). If you set up your will properly, most of your assets can go tax-free to your spouse and any amount under $675,000 (in 2000 and 2001) can be given to others without any tax liability. With this in mind, you should set up a will granting your spouse all assets over the $675,000 exclusion amount. Your spouse should do the same and grant you an identical amount. This way, whoever dies first can give the $675,000, tax-free, to anyone you want—your children, nephews and nieces, your bridge partner, or even your Newfoundland, for that matter—and the living spouse will get the rest, without incurring any tax liability. This structure is important because the $675,000 exclusion is a one-time deal, per person, for both you and your spouse. In other words, when the living spouse passes a way, a second exclusion of $675,000 is available. Essentially by structuring your will in this way, you've doubled your combined estate's available exclusion. Thus, although still a single estate, it now affords tax-free exclusions of $1.35 million.

The situation gets trickier if, after one spouse's death, the second remarries. In this scenario, the living spouse might not qualify for the $675,000 exclusion. Still, setting your will up in this fashion is one of the best safeguards against paying taxes on your assets upon your death, as well as a great way to keep your estate within the family. Remember, too, that once the second $675,000 has been distributed, the remaining assets will, in most cases, be subject to federal taxes. Even these taxes, however, can be mitigated to some degree, and I'll discuss below some aggressive tax-planning strategies to help in this regard.

Finally, when it comes to writing your will, be aware that using an attorney can be well worth the expense. Although you might be put off by the rates, they're actually quite reasonable, especially considering a well-written will is often offset by huge savings later on. You've probably seen "do-it-yourself" wills in books at local bookstores; these are generally only for the simplest of estates. If you want to take advantage of the strategies I'm discussing, you're better off hiring an attorney who specializes in will preparation.

# Using Your Residence For Tax Flexibility

As part of the Taxpayer Relief Act of 1997, the government changed some of the rules regarding your personal residence; most of these changes were to the taxpayers' advantage. The main advantage is that your residence can now be a tremendous vehicle for reducing your tax liability.

As of 1997, your home can appreciate in value by up to $500,000 (if you're married and filing jointly); every two years you can sell your home and not pay any taxes on gains up to this amount. Think about this: every four years you could make $1 million in sales of your residences without being liable for a dime of federal tax! This is a fantastic way to realize huge tax savings and at the same time use as an estate planning strategy.

The following is a scenario that would provide a way for you to buy a house, use it to increase your net worth and the value of your estate, not pay any taxes on the increase, and then pass the home on to your children without being subject to federal estate tax liability. Essentially, you would sell your house to your kids. Before doing that, however, you would put the house into an irrevocable trust. Then you would sell the house to you children. If your gain was less than $500,000 (married filing jointly—half that if you're single), you pay no taxes on that gain. Now, your children would own the home, and their tax basis for the house would be its value at the time you sold it to them. If they turned around immediately and sold the house for what they paid for it, they would have no tax liability on it. For example, if you bought a home ten years ago for $165,000, and today, it was worth $230,000, you could sell it to your kids for this amount; and this would become their basis. Remember, you wouldn't owe anything on your gain because it would be less than $500,000. Now let's say your children sold the home for $230,000; in so doing, they would incur no tax liability themselves.

What if you wanted to keep living in the house? No problem. You could stay right where you are, without moving a single couch or nightstand. You would simply pay rent to the new owners (your kids), thereby continuing to transfer tax-free money out of your estate. In fact, they could even write off part of the cost of the house as depreciation on a rental expense and show a loss on the house from rent they charge to you, as long as they are charging you a fair price.

In this scenario, there are several advantages. First, you unloaded your house and decreased the value of your estate while still maintaining a house to live in. Second, by paying rent, you continued to decrease the value of your estate, very likely resulting in paying no estate taxes whatsoever. Additionally, when, or if, they finally did sell the house, they'd probably not have a gain substantial enough to incur very high taxes. If, on the other hand, after you were gone they decided to live in the house, any appreciation on the house would be excludable to the same degree it was to you, as long as they lived in the house for the required two years.

## Passing On Commercial Property

Though commercial property passes on a little differently, there are strategies you can take advantage of here as well. Let's imagine for a moment that I'm a little older than I actually am right now, and I own a very large building that I would like to pass on to my children. I don't want to pay a huge chunk of money in taxes when I  make the transfer, whether I sell it or give it as a gift. Remember, as the owner of a personal residence, I'd be able to exclude up to $500,000 if I sold it.  I would have to make the transfer a little differently.  One way to do that would be to sell the property to my children but have them pay me back over time—essentially I would set up a private annuity by which they would make a certain number of fixed payments over the course of my lifetime in order to pay for the building.  Because I would not have seen the entire profit I'd made from the sale of this building, what would be my own tax liability then?  By using the installment sale method, I would calculate my profit based on the pro rata share of the capital gain and ordinary income received in the tax year. Then I would  pay tax on that share, not on the entire share at once.

For instance, let's say I bought a commercial building ten years ago for $200,000 and then sold it to my kids for $1 million. Today, in a sense, I've got an $800,000 capital-gain liability.  Since I'm not being paid the entire amount today, I'm only assessed a fraction of the full amount, perhaps one-twentieth of it, which is what my kids pay me a year for the property. When I die, if they decide they want to sell the property, their basis is going to be the amount for which the building was sold to them, not the amount for which I acquired it. That means I have increased the value of their estate without a substantial gain on their part, so they'd be avoiding those potentially massive taxes. At the same time, I'd be decreasing the value of my estate without paying gift taxes. Everyone comes out ahead—except the IRS.

# Giving It All Away

"I am to die broke," the crotchety old uncle of a friend of mine once said. And he did. Little did he know—or maybe he knew full well—the tax advantages he would enjoy. Remember that everyone gets an exemption of $10,000 for gifts to any individual within each calendar year. That means, if you've got five kids, you can give each of them that full amount, thereby reducing the value of your estate by $50,000 a year. And none of those gifts would be subject to federal estate or gift taxes. On top of that, your spouse is also allowed to give the same amount, and considering that her gift will probably come out of your estate anyway, that means the two of you have collectively reduced the value of your estate by $100,000.

I'm sure you may have heard or read somewhere about irrevocable trusts and living trusts. These types of funds—which are legally separate entities—offer certain advantages in some tax-case scenarios. In other cases they might not be the best way to go.

Let me talk first about irrevocable trusts. I've already discussed ways to pass on to your children, or other heirs, residential and commercial property. However, you might not feel comfortable doing that just yet. Perhaps your children are too young or haven't yet proved themselves responsible enough to control large amounts of money or property. Maybe you're not convinced yet that their judgment is sound enough to be caretakers of your assets. If so, irrevocable trusts might be your best bet. Irrevocable trusts are a terrific mechanism for passing on your assets—avoiding estate and gift taxes—while at the same time maintaining some control over them, ideally by appointing a trustee to actually control them. Whether there's cash, stocks, real property—whatever—a trustee of an irrevocable trust can make decisions that are in accordance with your wishes, as you've made clear, instead of in your children's, which might not be in their best interest in the long run.

Another advantage of the irrevocable trust is that it takes assets out of your name for legal purposes. We're all painfully aware that we live in a highly litigious time and place, and that excessive judgments for minor infractions seem common. Remember the case of the woman who went to McDonald's, put a cup of hot coffee between her legs, and drove off, spilled the coffee and then won a multi-million-dollar suit against McDonald's for their negligence? That's America for you: ski past an "out of bounds" sign at a ski resort, get hurt, and sue for damages. Break a leg falling through a skylight as you try to break into a building to rob it, and sue for damages. The point is that you don't want to have assets—especially ones that you don't need—that people can sue you for. Get them out of your name. Then, even if there is a judgment against you, the assets aren't available, because they're in a trust that is its own legal entity.

Living trusts are somewhat different from irrevocable trusts and are, in fact, more common. Designed essentially to avoid probate court, living trusts allow for the automatic transfer of your assets to your heirs at the time of your death, allowing for a far smoother period of transition. Unlike the irrevocable trust, your assets are still in your name until you die, and are therefore, fair game for creditors or judgments resulting from lawsuits. However, living trusts do provide a mechanism by which you can avoid some of the estate taxes that would otherwise be levied against you.

# Family Limited Partnerships

Still another way to reduce your taxable estate is by setting up what's known as a Family Limited Partnership. Let's say you started a business some twenty years ago and the business has grown to be quite successful. But for reasons I've discussed above, you'd like to get it out of your estate. Perhaps you'd like to give it to your children but are not comfortable letting them run things. Your desire is to hand it over to them for the purposes of estate planning and asset control, but still maintain control of the way the company does business.

A family limited partnership might be your answer because it allows you to give shares of your company to your children. Because the shares represent a minority position of the partnership, and are, by definition, worth less than controlling shares, they will have a discounted value for gift tax purposes. If you own 40% percent of the company and divide the remaining 60% equally among your three kids (20% of the company each), you then, are the company's general partner and have 100% control of the company. Your kids, as limited partners, have no control whatsoever. As the business grows and develops, your children will own that business, the property having been removed from the estate, and any appreciation between the time you gave it to them and the time you die will not be included in your estate because those shares in the company will have belonged to the children all along.

## Charitable-Remainder Trusts

Yet another way to reduce your assets for estate planning is to take advantage of the charitable-remainder trust. Imagine for a moment that you have some property that has gone up in value and you'd like to sell it. However, you're also looking at painfully high taxes on the gains. If one of your long-range goals is to donate some assets to your favorite charities when you die anyway, then you are a very good candidate for this kind of trust. By putting assets into a charitable-remainder trust, you get three things: first, you get a charitable deduction on your current tax return equal to the present value of the asset which you put into the trust. Second, you still own the asset and you don't pay any tax on the gain because the money is in the trust for the benefit of the charity. Third, you can actually take income out of the trust periodically, and though you would pay taxes on it, at least it's available to you for day-to-day living or other expenses that come up. In fact, in some cases, you can take a rather large chunk of income out a charitable-remainder trust, and even though you pay taxes on it, you've already enjoyed the benefit of the earlier deduction, and not paid tax on any gain you might have realized from sale of the asset.

## A Final Word on Estate Planning

Estate planning is very complicated. I must emphasize that I'm offering only the broadest of overviews. You need to make use of the services of a professional if you plan to set up any of these plans. Books are available, of course, but the relatively nominal fee you pay a professional today could pay for itself ten or a hundred fold in twenty years when all the positioning and structuring you've done really matters. Though there are many qualified and honest professionals out there, there are also plenty of flakes and quacks. Before you hire someone, get referrals. Ask your colleagues whom they've used. Check with your local Better Business Bureau. Meet with attorneys and consultants you might end up using before committing yourself  because it's important that the person whose services you use is not only qualified and honest, but also someone with whom you get along personally. If possible, you should not only respect, but also like each other.  Do it right the first time and you won't end up doing it again.

As always, you're probably tired of reading by now, keep accurate and up-to-date records. Keep not only the paperwork these trusts generate, but keep logs of your discussions with the professionals you hire. Also, keep track of the conversations you have with your children about the trusts and the roles they will play when you die. Make sure they know where the money and assets are and who the executors and trustees are. Do this in writing with your children, even if official paperwork notifies them of the same thing. Write to that oldest daughter and let her know she now owns 30% of your company and what that means, and get the letter notarized. Remember, it's far better to over-document than to under-document.

# Chapter Thirteen

# Other Useful Deductions

*"Ah, it's a lovely thing to know a thing or two."*
**-Moliere, *Le Bourgeois Gentilhomme***

*"I only ask for information."*
**-Charles Dickens, *David Copperfield***

So far, I've been talking mostly about deductions for companies and other ways business owners can reduce their tax liability. I've also discussed ways individuals can start businesses to better take advantage of what's available. There are a whole slew of miscellaneous deductions available to business owners and individuals. These deductions don't fit into any of the categories covered so far. Remember that the United States Tax Code is 6,000 pages long! Buried in those pages and within that somewhat indecipherable language is a lot of valuable information. Though getting to know that Tax Code might seem daunting, the better informed you are, the better your chances are of reducing your tax liability and saving big money.

This chapter will also cover some of the common pitfalls that many American taxpayers face and teach you how to avoid them yourself. At the same time, I'll be emphasizing the value of playing by the rules established by the Internal Revenue Service and our country's judiciary. That way, if you ever are audited, you'll pass with flying colors.

## Interest on Student Loans

Recently, I had a transcription service transcribe some tapes I'd recorded for a lecture series. At one point, the woman who was doing the transcription came to me laughing. "You know," she said, "just listening to your tapes I've figured out how to deduct about $1,500 for my son this year." I asked her what she was talking about. "That student loan stuff," she said. "How he should start paying interest on his student loans now because he's got to pay it eventually anyway. I didn't realize he could deduct that interest. That's going to give him a huge tax break." I looked at her and smiled. "Good. Then I won't pay you for transcribing my tapes and we'll call it even." She smiled back, but didn't think it was as funny as I did.

Interest on student loans is something you should look into as far as deductions. You can deduct up to $2500 of interest paid on qualified educational "student" loans. The deduction starts to phase out once your adjusted gross income reaches $50,000 (filing single) or $100,000 (married, filing jointly).

## Tax Credits

If you have dependent children, whether they are newborn or just starting their higher education (or if your are, for that matter), there are several tax credits about which you should be aware. Tax credits are actually more beneficial than tax deductions, because they come right off your tax liability. While tax deductions affect your adjusted gross income, tax credits come right off the amount you owe.

Historically there have always been exemptions for

dependent children. For years, as long as you filled out a Form SS-5 and got a Social Security number for your child, he or she was a legitimate exemption. As of 1998, however, there are also available tax credits for parents. For 2002, that amount is $600 per child; and again, it is deducted directly from the tax amount the IRS says you owe. The bad news here is that the child tax credit is phased out after income levels of $110,000 (2002, filing jointly).

Another particularly attractive tax credit for parents is the Hope Scholarship credit. This is a credit for tuition and related expenses for each student enrolled in a post-secondary institution. Created by the Taxpayer Relief Act of 1997, the Hope Scholarship Credit was designed to help make more affordable two years of your children's college or certificate education. Annual available credits are 100% of the first $1,000 in tuition and fees and 50% of the next $1,000. That's $1,500 you can subtract from your total tax bill! Note that the credit is phased out at between $41,000 and $51,000 (adjust gross income, filing singly) or between $82,000 and $102,000 (married, filing jointly).

Another option is the Lifetime Learning Credit, which is a tax credit equal to up to 20% of the first $5,000 in expenses for higher education. Again, this is a $1,000 credit subtracted directly from the taxes you owe. Remember, unlike the Hope Scholarship, the Lifetime Learning Credit is only available once per family, not to each child/student in that family. Keep in mind, too, that you cannot use both the Hope Scholarship and the Lifetime Learning credits in the same year. Let's say you have a daughter who is college-bound next fall. You might want to use the Lifetime Learning Credit the first year and the Hope Scholarships the subsequent two years. Now you're looking at as much as $2,500 in tax credits in the first three years of your daughter's post-secondary education.    Finally, remember that not all institutions of higher learning are accredited for these two credits.   As you kids are researching different colleges, factor that  information into the final decision.

One tax credit that's especially useful for low-income taxpayers is the earned-income credit.  The amount for which you qualify depends on your annual salary and the number of your dependents.  Instead of waiting to reap the benefit of this credit when you file your return, file a form W-5 with your employer, who will add a portion of your earned-income credit to your weekly paycheck. It's like I always say:  why let the government use your money interest-free all year long, when you could give yourself an immediate pay raise?

## Coverdell Education Savings Accounts

In 1997 Congress created the Educational IRAs to help families save for college. The only problem was these accounts could barely cover the cost of parking at a university let alone tuition and books. So in 2001, Congress overhauled these accounts and renamed them Coverdell Education Savings Accounts (CESA).   These accounts work much like the Roth IRA. The contribution is made after tax (you don't get a tax deduction for the annual contribution), however, the earnings are distributed tax free to the student once they are in college or university.

An account can be set-up for anyone under age 18. The maximum contribution to the account is $2000 per year and it is considered a gift so it is not taxable to the beneficiary. A student can draw down the account to cover qualified expenses like books and tuition and the distribution is normally tax-free. The only thing to watch out for is that you cannot take a tax-free distribution and a Hope or Lifetime Learning Credit in the same year.

## More About Roth IRAs

Also covered in Chapter 11, Roth IRAs are currently one of the best available retirement accounts. As with Education IRAs, your contributions are made with taxable monies; they are not deductions. However, when you draw payments from the account in your retirement, the money is then tax-free.

This could end up making a huge difference in your post-retirement income. Imagine the enormous amount that could be distributed to your retirement if, starting at age 30, you put $250 (there's an annual maximum of $3,000) of your $4,000-a-month salary into a Roth IRA and then after retiring were able to draw $2,500 a month tax-free (which is, perhaps, added to your $2,000 company pension). Not bad, I'd say, and most tax experts agree that the tax-free status of the withdrawals easily offset the taxed contributions. Depending on what that money did while it was in the Roth IRA, it could be put it in mutual funds, individual stocks, bonds, whatever you choose, at   retirement, you could be taking surprisingly big withdrawals that, again, are absolutely tax-free. Another advantage of the Roth IRA is that there are certain expenses that qualify for no-penalty withdrawals, such as the purchase of a first home.

The minimum age at which you can begin drawing from your

Roth IRA is 59 1/2, and you only need to have paid into your Roth IRA for five years before you're vested in it (able to withdraw without penalty). Additionally, phase-out limits by income amount are quite high on Roth IRAs: between $95,000 – $110,000 if you're filing singly, $150,000 – $160,000 if you're married and filing jointly. The contribution limit for a Roth IRA is $3,000 and another $3,000 for a non-working spouse.

## Conventional IRAs

Individual retirement accounts have been around for a long time, and although they might not have the novel appeal of Roth and Education IRAs, they're a great resource for saving money on taxes. Their main attraction is that you can put money into them now in such a way as to lower your tax liability. In other words, if your adjusted gross income were $5,000 a month, you would be taxed at year's end based on $60,000. If your tax rate were 30%, you'd be paying $18,000 in taxes. If, however, you could afford to put $500 a month (the annual maximum is $6,000) into an IRA, you would have reduced your taxable income to $54,000. That same 30% would then equal $16,200. On top of the $1800 you saved on taxes, you would have $6,000 in an account that you had invested in stocks, mutual funds, bonds, or even a conservative savings account. At the end of the year, that $6,000 could be worth well more than you paid into it.

By starting young enough, you can ride out the market's ups and downs, knowing full well that in the long run your money will grow. There's nothing quite like opening that quarterly statement from your investment and seeing that your IRA has been earning 17%

interest for you. Unlike the Roth IRA, once you begin taking money out of a conventional IRA, you then must pay taxes on it. The theory is that, once you've retired, you will be in a much lower tax bracket and will therefore have to pay less in taxes.

## Medical Expenses

Talk to anyone with decent employer-supplied medical insurance, and she'll most likely tell you it's one of the best parts about the job. In fact, many people stay at their jobs primarily because of the medical insurance included in their benefit plan. Conversely, talk to anyone who's self-employed, and most likely one of his biggest gripes will be that he has to pay for his own medical insurance, which, as we all know, is exorbitantly expensive. You could very easily pay between two and four hundred dollars or more for a mediocre insurance policy, for which you might have co-pays on office visits, emergency-room visits, prescriptions, and other incidental expenses. That would be if you're a low-risk customer and have neither children nor pre-existing medical conditions. By adding in any of those factors, you could easily pay substantially more for a decent policy.

You're probably aware that you can legally write off medical expenses that are in excess of 7 1/2% of your adjusted gross income. What would some of those expenses be? Things like prescription drugs, your son's hospital stay,  and an emergency trip to the dentist when your daughter broke a tooth skateboarding are classical medical deductions that will in no way give the IRS pause.

There are many treatments and expenses that you have every

year that you may not realize are deductible medical expenses. Anything that is recommended by a doctor can qualify towards the 7 1/2%. Items such as nutritional supplements, vitamins, acupuncture, and chiropractic could all be included. In order for these expenses to qualify as deductible, all you need is a note from your doctor saying they were medically necessary. For example, suppose you have rheumatoid arthritis that causes great pain to your joints. If a weekly massage helps ease that pain, and you can get a note from your doctor—not a prescription, just a note—indicating that the treatment does in fact help, then those expenses are in fact deductible, or at least applicable toward your 7 1/2% ceiling.

Additional procedures and programs whose expenses might be deductible include sterilization (vasectomies, for instance), substance-abuse programs, and medical fees associated with college tuition. In fact, when I was in college, I was required to pay a monthly fee to the university clinic as part of my tuition. While I couldn't write off the whole tuition, I could (and did) write off the portion for the clinic. Once you begin adding up these miscellaneous expenses, you might be amazed. They could quickly result in thousands of dollars of savings for your family, money that could be going toward vacations, investments, even retirement.

Note that in some cases, married couples can take better advantage of the deductions allowed for medical expenses by filing their taxes separately. This is especially true if one spouse is making significantly more money than the other. Let's say spouse Number 1 makes $80,000, and spouse Number 2 makes $15,000. If spouse Number 1 claimed the deductions, the 7 1/2% rule wouldn't kick in until the expenses totaled $6,000. On the other hand, if spouse Number 2 claimed the deductions, the rule would kick in when expenses totaled $1,225.

## Casualty Losses

I am frequently amazed by the number of people with casualty losses who don't write them off. Perhaps they don't realize that the government allows them to, or perhaps they're intimidated by the admittedly (and typically) overly complex rules. In layman's terms, you can basically write off any amount of the value of a loss of an asset that's over 10% of your adjusted gross income (AGI), plus a flat $100 per casualty.

This is how it works: let's say you have a garage worth $50,000, and that garage catches on fire and burns to the ground. The insurance company only compensates you $25,000 for your loss. Your casualty loss would then be $25,000 on the garage. Now, if your AGI is $70,000, then 10% of your AGI is $7,000. Subtract that $7,000 from your $25,000 loss, and you have $18,000 (minus $100) that you can write off. Here is another example: we recently had a client who purchased a brand-new recreational vehicle and decided to use it to take some friends to a football game. Well, on the way, they spilled drinks all over the carpet. The estimate to replace it was $3,500. (The RV was so new he hadn't even purchased insurance yet.) Of course he was upset until NADN pointed out to him that the cost of replacing the carpet was a casualty loss even if he never replaced the carpet. All he was required to do was provide a couple of estimates from carpet repair companies and then use a reasonable figure as the basis of his loss. Now, he might in fact make more than $35,000 so that expense wouldn't be deductible all by itself.

However, once he added up all his casualty losses for the year, he was then able to deduct everything that was over 10% of his AGI.

In conclusion, if you make, say $60,000, you can write off any amount that totals over $6,000, minus $100. As with allowable deductions for medical expenses, casualty losses can sometimes be better taken advantage of if you and your spouse file your taxes separately, especially if you make significantly different amounts of money. Since the person making less can claim the loss, you will arrive at the 10% figure sooner and will thus be able to claim more deductions.

## Deductions For Traveling Between Job Sites

In general, you cannot deduct expenses incurred commuting from your home to your office. However, there are ways to structure and define the work you do so that some job-related travel expenses do become deductible.

I discussed in great detail in Chapter 7 about the advantages of operating a business out of your home; one of the best advantages is claiming the many possible deductions. For example, if you have a home office and travel from it to another business location, that mileage is deductible, precisely because the Internal Revenue Service does not consider it "commuting." You can either use the IRS-allowable rate for the year 2002 of 36.5 cents per mile or you can itemize your actual expenses; this is generally a far better method.

Now, let's say you have a home-based business and work a few hours every morning before heading off to your other job. If, along the way, or when you arrived at your other job, you dropped off a few business cards or otherwise made attempts to increase the profit objective of your home business, then you would in fact be traveling from one business to another, and your mileage would be deductible.

Remember, too, that travel to a temporary site is tax deductible. That is, if you spend one week of the year at one job site, two weeks at another, and three at still another, then your travel back and forth between these sites would in fact qualify as tax-deductible, job-related travel. Let's say that you work for a chain of stores, and that you normally work in Store A. However, every once in a while, you are transferred to Store B, C, or D. In that case, traveling to at least one of these other stores would be a tax-deductible expense for you. Some other examples of tax-deductible traveling expenses would be if you work two separate jobs, traveling between them would be deductible. If you travel for charitable activities, you can deduct 14 cents per mile. If you travel for medical reasons, you can deduct 13 cents per mile.

Fourteen cents per mile here and 13 cents per mile there probably don't sound like very much. However, little expenses add up—as you well know from making them in the first place. Miles add up quickly, too. Just consider how quickly you drive 300 miles between gas station fill-ups. Now imagine being able to write off a good portion of those miles.

Finally, remember, it's absolutely critical to keep receipts, and a log of all the traveling you do. If your records are in good order, you will most likely come out of any audit smelling like a rose. If all you've got are a bunch of receipts stuffed into a shoebox, and a vague notion—nothing in writing—of where you traveled or for what reasons, you're a sitting duck as far as the Internal Revenue Service is concerned. Not keeping records, or not keeping them in a presentable fashion could not only cost you the deductions, but could also mean penalties.

## Traveling to Look For Work

People change jobs today far more frequently than folks did in the past. A generation ago, it was the rule with few exceptions, that once someone was hired by a company or state agency, it was likely that he or she would stay there until retirement. Even if they did change firms, they most often would not move geographically very far away. Things are different today. As kids graduate from college and looking for their "first job," they might stay there for five years or so and then move on, often in the same general field. Since distance travel is so convenient these days, it's not unusual that after learning the ropes at a firm in New Jersey, a person may move across the country to Silicon Valley and join an up-and-coming dot-com company. In fact, professional "headhunters" actively seek out qualified personnel who work at one firm and try to seduce them to leave to go to work for another. If you do decide you want to quit your job, move to another city, and go to work for someone new, you're going to have to visit the area in which you plan to move. In fact, you might end up visiting several different cities as you talk to potential employers.

The Internal Revenue Service allows deductions for this kind of travel. As long as you're looking for work in the same field in which you're already employed, a trip in search of work is deductible (subject to the 2% AGI floor). That means, a realtor could take a trip to Hawaii, put an application in with realty offices there and write off the trip. He couldn't so that, however, if he were looking for a "career change." He couldn't write off a trip if he were looking for work as a tour boat guide. It is important to remember that you can only deduct the expenses relating to finding a new job if you are currently employed. The IRS will generally disallow deductions for job seeking travel if you have been unemployed for a period of time.

*Note:* There might not actually be much of your type of work available where you take your trip, but it's certainly worth filling out some applications and putting out some feelers.

# Chapter Fourteen

# Answers to Some Common Questions

*"Be not forgetful to entertain strangers."*
**-James 13:1, *The Bible***

"The same judges reach different conclusions on familiar issues. A court will ignore a wild motion or appeal for years, then one day embrace it and grant relief. Judges die and they're replaced by judges who think differently. Presidents come and go and they appoint their pals to the bench. The Supreme Court drifts one way, then another."

**-John Grisham, *The Chamber***

It's no wonder that American taxpayers get confused about what deductions they can and can't take or what credits they are or are not eligible for in their income bracket. Ceilings for credits go up and then they come down. It seems that rules and regulations are revised by the IRS and re-interpreted by the courts almost daily. At the writing of this book, the entire package of business expenses (travel, entertainment, meals) and deductions is undergoing review with an eye toward revisions. No one knows for certain what tomorrow will bring. However, with an eye on what the laws and rules are today, this chapter brings together the most frequently asked questions we receive at the National Audit Defense Network.

# General Questions

### What's the difference between a tax credit and a tax deduction?

A tax credit is an allowance that is subtracted directly from the amount of taxes you owe. Examples include credit for dependent children, as well as certain scholarship funds. A deduction, on the other hand, is an allowance that is subtracted from your income to compute your taxable income. For example, let's say your income for a given year was $50,000 and you owed $18,000 in federal taxes. A tax credit of $2,000 would be subtracted directly from that $18,000, while a tax deduction of $2,000 would be subtracted from the $50,000, which, ultimately, would change the amount you owe but that difference would not amount to $2,000. You can see, then, that credits are generally worth more than deductions.   For more information, see Chapter 13 or the Glossary.

### How do I ensure I'm correctly filling out all those confusing IRS forms?

Hire a professional.  Currently, the United States Tax Code is over 6,000 pages long, and although it's readily available online, it's very difficult to make much sense of it. That, coupled with the complexity of the IRS forms, (and it's quite likely your return could include a dozen or more of them) means you just might get very frustrated trying to understand what you're filing.  If you don't know what you're doing, there's a very good chance that you're not taking advantage of all the deductions, credits, and exclusions you're allowed.  It makes good sense to pay someone to help you.  A good CPA or other professional tax preparer will very likely save you more money than you pay him for his services.

**How do I write off medical expenses?**

The IRS allows you to write off any medical expenses in excess of 7 1/2% of your Adjusted Gross Income (AGI) if you itemize your deductions.  These expenses include everything from prescription drugs to medical stays, as well as procedures your doctor recommends in writing, even if he or she doesn't technically prescribe them.  These can include massage, acupuncture, nutritional supplements, vitamins, even such things as vasectomies and treatment at substance-abuse clinics.  For more information, see Chapter 13.

**Can I write off a trip to an area where I have rental property?**

Yes, you can.  If you are responsible for the maintenance and repair of the property, and you collect the rent checks yourself, then you can write off the expenses incurred when you travel to the property.  It doesn't matter if you are going there to simply check on the property, do repairs, compare values of similar property in determining rent amounts, or network with other merchants and property owners in the area.  As long as you maintain responsibility for the property and have not hired a management/maintenance company, your travel expenses are tax deductible.

If your rental property is maintained by a property-management company however, you can still write off travel that has the express purpose of ensuring that the company is doing its job properly—keeping the lawn mowed, the tenants happy, etc.
For more information, see Chapter 5.

**Can I access my personal retirement account without paying penalties for early withdrawal?**

It depends wholly on what type of retirement account you have and what you intend to use the money for. This is why it's critical that you look closely at and understand completely what type of account it is. For example, if you have a Roth IRA, from which you ordinarily wouldn't be able to draw funds until you were 59 1/2 years of age, you can take money without penalty for specific uses, such as education and the first-time purchase of a home up to $10,000. For more information, see Chapter 11.

**What are my actual chances of being audited?**

This is a difficult question to answer, as your chances depend to a large degree on the part of the country in which you live and what kind of return you're filing. In very general terms, your chances of being audited are greater if you live in the western United States and are operating a corporation with an annual income of over $100,000. However, even where your chances of being audited are greatest, they are still less than 2.5%. For more information, see Chapters 15 and 17.

# Questions That Affect Your Family

**Is it better to file joint or separate to avoid the so-called "marriage penalty" tax?**

The marriage penalty essentially means that spouses with separate incomes will pay more tax by filing jointly than they would pay if they were to file as two single taxpayers. For example, in 2001, the standard deduction for a married couple filing jointly was $7,600. The standard deduction for a single taxpayer was $4,550. If the couple were able to take advantage of a joint single deduction, they would have been able to take a standard deduction of $9,100. Translated into real dollars, the marriage penalty works out to be $225 if you are in the 15% bracket and $420 if you are in the 28% bracket. As your income increases, so does the "penalty." Depending on your income, this penalty can rise to well over $1,000.

When deciding how to file, there are a number of things you need to keep in mind. By filing jointly, although you have a bit of a penalty, you are able to take certain credits and deductions that you cannot take if you file separately. For example, you can only take the Earned Income Tax Credit (EITC) if you file jointly. Other tax benefits that would be limited by a separate filing include:

- Credit for the Elderly and Disabled
- Child Care Credit
- Hope Scholarship Credit
- Lifetime Learning Credit
- Student Loan Interest Deduction
- Spousal IRA Deduction
- Capital Loss Deduction
- Exclusion of Gain on the Sale of Principle Residence

Although there is a marriage penalty, the loss of deductions and credits outweighs the additional burden of the marriage penalty. There are still some reasons why someone might choose to file separately such as by doing so, it separates the spousal tax liability. This is usually important when a marriage is in a dissolution phase and both spouses are separating their marital property. It is also beneficial on your state tax return in certain states and, in some rare occasions, some couples actually pay less tax if they file separately.

**If filing separately, can one spouse take all the mortgage interest and real estate taxes? Is there a rule on who claims the children?**

Each spouse can deduct the expenses they paid for themselves. If the funds used to pay these expenses were from a joint account, then each spouse would deduct 1/2 of the expenses. One note of caution, the law requires that each spouse use the same method for calculating deductions. If one spouse itemizes, then both must itemize even if that means that one spouse had less in deductions than their standard deduction.

When dealing with dependents, remember that a dependent can only be claimed on one return. You can take a qualified dependent on a return so long as the person claiming them provides more than 50% of their total support for the year. If you are filing separately, it is important that you coordinate with your spouse and make a decision as to which one of you will be taking which dependent.

**Other than the normal dependency deductions, are there other deductions or credits available to families with children?**

There are four main credits available to families with qualifying children. As with all credits in the tax law, certain income phase-out rules apply to each of these credits, and of course, they are subject to change every year. So make certain you speak to your tax professional before using them. The four tax credits are:

1. Child Tax Credit: This $600 per-child credit is available to taxpayers with a qualifying child who is under 17 years of age on December 31. One note of caution, the child must be a US citizen in order to be eligible for the credit.

2. Child and Dependent Care Credit: This is a nonrefundable credit allowed for a  portion of a qualifying child or dependent's care expenses paid for the purpose of allowing the taxpayer to be gainfully employed. It is claimed on the Form 2441 and the taxpayer must maintain the household in order to be eligible for the credit.

3. Earned Income Tax Credit:  This is a refundable tax credit designed to give taxpayers with children who make below an income threshold amount, extra money to help raise their family. The credit is only available to taxpayers who are employed and have earned income.

4. Credits for Higher Education Tuition: These credits are available to low and middle-income taxpayers for tuition expenses incurred by student's pursuing college or graduate degrees. They are broken down into two categories: the Hope credit and the Lifetime Learning Credit. The Hope credit is specifically designed to give credits to families who have students in attending college for their freshman and sophomore years. The lifetime learning credit gives a tax credit of 20% for up to $5000 of qualified educational expenses, no matter when they occur in a taxpayer's educational career. For more information, see Chapter 13.

## For non-custodial parents paying child support, what tax benefits are available?

That depends partly on what year your divorce was final.  If you were divorced prior to 1985, the law grants the non-custodial parent the exemption provided they are paying at least $600 in annual support.   If your divorce was after 1985, generally the custodial parent gets to claim the child.   Increasingly though, courts are including specific language allocating the dependent exemptions in the divorce decree.

The IRS has begun a program to crack down on divorced parents both claiming the same child.   If you are the non-custodial parent and you are claiming the exemption, you must have the custodial parent complete and sign a Form 8332 Release of Claim and attach it to your return. That way, there is no dispute as to who has the right to claim a child.   If both of you claim the child, your returns will be audited and the IRS will disallow the exemption on both returns until a legal basis can be claimed by either of the parents. Let me also clarify one point.   Child support is never tax deductible. Only alimony can be deducted from your income.

**How can a multiple support agreement provide tax breaks?**

A multiple support agreement is used when two or more individuals collectively provide more than 1/2 of the support of a qualifying dependent. Since only one person may claim a dependent for any tax year, each person not claiming the dependent must complete and sign a Form 2120 then attach it to the return of the person claiming the dependent. These agreements typically come into play when two or more siblings are caring for elderly parents. Neither can claim the dependency deduction based on their own contributions towards their parents' care and support so an agreement can be made allowing each sibling to claim the dependent in alternating years. The real benefit is that it allows a caregiver to have some tax relief in alternating years with their co-caregiving siblings.

**What is a form 8332?  What role does it play in saving on taxes?**

Form 8332, Release of Claim to Exemption for Child of Divorced or Separated Parents, is used when the non-custodial parent of a child is allowed to claim the child as an exemption in one year or all future tax years.  For purposes of our discussion, the non-custodial parent is the one who had the child for a short period of time during the year while the custodial parent had the child for the majority of the time.  While there are a multitude of child custody arrangements, the IRS is looking at time spent physically in a household and the source of support for the child in determining the dependency exemption.  If you are in a situation where there is no divorce decree, then the parent who has the child physically residing with them for more than six months can take the deduction.

**Can you claim children as dependents if they live abroad?**

Interesting question. We are seeing more and more people supporting family members abroad while living in the United States. Unfortunately, under current tax law, you can only claim a dependent living in either Canada or Mexico on your federal income tax.  In order to claim that dependent you will have to obtain a taxpayer identification number for them issued by the U.S. Government. Unless that person is a U.S. citizen and eligible to obtain a social security number, you will have to obtain an ITIN, a number issued by the IRS to foreign nationals ineligible for a social security number so that they can be claimed on a U.S. tax return. You can obtain that number by completing a Form W-7 and mailing it to the IRS. Once you have received an ITIN number for a qualifying dependent living in Mexico or Canada, you can claim them on your return.

**Is there still a tax credit for adopting a child?**

Yes.    You can still claim a non-refundable tax credit for adopting a child. There are different rules as to when expenses can be recognized for purposes of claiming the credit, but the general rules apply to all situations.  The credit is for an amount up to $10,000 of qualified adoption expenses.    These include all reasonable and necessary adoption fees, court costs, attorney fees and other expenses which are directly related to the legal adoption of an eligible child. An eligible child is defined as one who has not reached the age of 18 as of the time of the adoption or who is physically or mentally incapable of caring for himself. Once you have finalized the adoption, you may also be eligible for all of the other credits available to taxpayers with qualifying children.

# Questions That Affect Your Business

**Can I claim the home office deductions even if I'm rarely in the office?**

Absolutely.    Until recently, a home office was defined as a "principal place of business."    However, the Internal Revenue Service recently came to understand that some business people who need to keep home offices spend most of their working time away from them.  For example, if you're an electrical contractor, you will need to maintain a home office for your records, for billing, for doing phone and online ordering of parts, etc., but most of your work time will be spent in the field.  You can still claim expenses incurred for the purposes of setting up and maintaining that home office.  For more information, see Chapter 6.

**How long should I keep my receipts and records from past years?**

Generally, the Internal Revenue Service can audit you for up to three years after you file your return. Beyond that, they're not supposed to be able to audit you unless they suspect fraud. Sometimes though, the IRS goes back five or six years and says, "Okay, prove x, y, and z." Well, you've thrown away all the records, because the three years have passed. Does that stop the Internal Revenue Service? Not in the least. All they have to do is prove civil fraud. And if you've thrown away all your records, you're going to have a difficult time proving you were on the up-and-up.

*Note:* There are consequences for discarding some types of business records, such as stocks, bonds, and real estate. For example, you'd need to keep the information from a real-estate transaction to justify its actual cost in order to indicate gains and losses.

*Note:* What is the bottom line? I recommend keeping your records seven years, or even longer. After all, they don't take up all that much room, and they'd sure be nice to have should you ever need them. For more information, see Chapter 7.

**Do I need to keep all my receipts?**

Technically, no; for practical purposes, yes. The Internal Revenue Service asks for receipts for expenses over certain amounts—for example, $75 in the case of business trip meals—and technically, you don't need to have a receipt to document an expense less than that amount. In reality, though, you're much better off having all your receipts. If you can show an auditor that your documentation is in good order, and you've actually done more than the IRS requires, your chances of winning that audit increase dramatically. For more information, see Chapter 7.

**Do I need any documentation of expenses besides my receipts?**

The best complement to your receipts is a log or diary of expenses. If you're audited and have claimed, for example, a $95 dinner as a business expense and all you have is a receipt, you're not going to appear very professional. However, if along with that receipt you have a daily log and are able to match the date on the receipt to the date of an entry, you will be able to make a much stronger case for the legitimacy of that expense, (i.e. "Dinner with Mr. Sanders, talked about ways to increase distribution channels...").

You should also use your diary log to keep track of travel and business expenses. In addition, if you have a home office at which you see clients, customers, or patients, be sure to have them sign a log or record of some time when they meet with you there. Keeping a professional log that will impress the IRS is neither complicated nor time consuming and could end up saving you thousands of dollars in the long run. Other useful pieces of documentation include canceled checks, phone bills, photographs, etc. For more information, see Chapter 7.

**To what amount can I write off improvements to the rest of my house if I have a home office?**

Basically, any improvement, including maintenance, can be deducted to the degree that your home office is a percentage of the square footage of your home. For example, if your home is 2,000 square feet and you're home office is 300 square feet, then you can deduct 15% of most any expense the house incurs, including services and purchases. For example, you can deduct 15% of the costs of house cleaning, lawn maintenance, pest control, window washing, painting, etc. Additionally, you can deduct 15% of the costs of new windows, carpeting, a lawn mower, etc.  Remember, this is in addition to the 15% you deduct from utilities, such as gas and electricity, as well as the 100% of the expenses directly related to your office, such as a desk, pencil sharpener, dictionary, electric stapler, and file cabinet.  For more information, see Chapter 8.

### Can I write off expenses such as the cost of swimming-pool service?

That would depend on the degree to which you can make a case that the pool plays a part in your profit motive.  If, for example, you entertain clients in your backyard pool, then by all means the costs of maintaining the pool may be partially deductible. For more information, see Chapter 8.

### Should I take the 36.5 cents IRS mileage allowance or itemize my vehicle expenses?

It depends on which amounts to more.  I recommend keeping your receipts for gas, tires, oil changes, etc, and then comparing their totals at the end of the year with the amount the IRS allows.  Keep in mind, however, that the 36.5 cents-per-mile deduction is probably low.  Rental-car companies have published reports saying they often spend as much as 50 cents to $1.00 per mile on their cars—and that's with their fleet discounts for parts and service.  The reality is, maintaining a vehicle in good working order could run anywhere from 75 cents to a dollar a mile.  For more information, see Chapter 8.

### Can I take my spouse on a business trip and write off the expenses?

Yes. There are two ways of looking at this. You can bring

along a spouse who doesn't work for you and write off any expenses you'd incur if you were going alone. For example, you could write off your accommodations, because you'd have to sleep somewhere anyway, and usually, there's no extra charge for a second person if he or she sleeps in the same bed. If there is an extra charge, say the hotel charges an additional $10, you can write off all but that additional $10.

The second thing you can do is to hire your spouse to do legitimate work for you, in which case you can write off 100% of his or her expenses. For more information, see Chapter 8.

### Can I combine business and personal travel and write off my expenses?

If you structure your traveling within the parameters defined by the Internal Revenue Service, you can write off a substantial percentage of your travel expenses. Additionally, you can enjoy many of the luxuries of a personal vacation while you're on a business-related trip. In fact, you might even be able to plan a vacation so that it actually becomes a business trip. Keep in mind the differences between what the IRS calls travel expenses and transportation expenses. Transportation expenses include those incurred getting you to and from your destination. Travel expenses include those incurred in your day-to-day living while you're on your trip. For more information, see Chapter 8.

### Can I hire my young children to work for me?

Yes, if your children are at least seven years old and you've got a sole proprietorship or an S corporation, you can hire them at a fair prevailing wage to do legitimate work for you. In fact, you can pay them up to $4,550 each per year, money that comes directly off your tax liability. You can also hire your spouse and other family members, but only to do legitimate work for a fair and reasonable wage. For more information see Chapter 8.

### Do I have to have a profitable business in order to claim deductions?

No. In fact, when your business isn't showing a profit is a time you should aggressively seek ways to reduce your tax liability, and one of the best ways to do so is by deducting expenses. Let's say you've started a house-painting business. Obviously it's going to cost a lot to establish yourself. You need to buy a truck (or trucks), compressors, spray guns, brushes, and rollers, and you need to invest money in getting the word out that you're ready to do business. You'll need business cards, a separate phone line, ads in local newspapers and the yellow pages. You might even want to get a sign painted on your truck. These are all expenses you can write off whether you are showing a profit or not, and since you probably won't have a huge client base right away, it's very likely that you'll be showing a loss, at least that first year. Remember, too, that all those expenses are what the Internal Revenue Service expects you to incur, as you establish your "profit motive." For more information, see Chapter 6.

### How many years will the IRS allow me to show losses?

The general rule is three years. That is, once you start up your business, the Internal Revenue Service generally gives you three years to show a profit. After that, they'll start looking at your return, and you'll increase your chances of being audited. However, as important as showing a profit that fourth year is, being able to prove you were making every attempt to is just as important. When the IRS comes knocking, you need to be able to show you have a legitimate "profit motive" or "profit objective." This is documentation demonstrating that the genuine purpose of your company is indeed to make money.  Many companies, large and small, have written off losses for more than three years.  For more information, see Chapter 6.

**To what degree must I disclose my involvement in a corporation?**

It depends on what that involvement is, but generally, you need not disclose the involvement at all.  That is, the corporation is an entirely separate entity.  For example, on your individual tax return you're not legally responsible for indicating that you have assets in that corporation.  For more information, see Chapter 9.

# Chapter Fifteen

# The IRS and You

*"Good God prepare me!"*
**-Samuel Pepys' last words**

*"All the people like us are We....and everyone else are They."*
**-Rudyard Kipling,** *We and They*

"Audit." If you're like most Americans, just the sound of the word makes the hair on the back of your neck stand up and your stomach feel like you've just swallowed a roll of quarters. Why does even the most honest, conservative filer still feel terror at the thought of being audited? Perhaps because the horror stories are legendary. You've probably heard or read accounts like the following: "Taxpayers making one-cent errors and being fined thousands of dollars," "IRS agents targeting and auditing people against whom they have personal vendetta,." "The IRS seizes property needed for folks' very survival," "Agents have quotas," and "The IRS pays informants who report suspected cheats", etc. Some of the stories may be exaggerated. Studies show, however, that fear of the IRS is indeed justified; there are vast inconsistencies in the way tax returns are dealt with, how audits are carried out, and how fines are levied. The audit as defined by the Internal Revenue Service is an "impartial review of the taxpayer's return to determine its completeness and accuracy." If only it were that simple. Studies show that death and

IRS audits are the two things that Americans fear most. Despite the stories, the reality is that an audit should not be something about which to be overly concerned. On the other hand, you should know what your chances of being audited are, what will happen in the event that you are audited, and just what your rights and recourses are.

First of all, if you plan to take advantage of the tax strategies I've laid out in this book, there will be at least a chance you will be audited by the Internal Revenue Service. Remember, simply operating a home business alerts the IRS that you are most likely claiming certain (legal) deductions, and are making every attempt to pay as little in taxes as you legally can. What's more, the IRS might go so far as to assume that you've started your home business not to legitimately make money or provide a service, but instead to solely reduce your tax liability.

Keep in mind that, in general, your chances of being audited increase as your annual income increases. Among people filing 1040 forms in 1995, fewer than 1% of those making $25,000-$50,000 were audited, while almost 3% of those making over $100,000 were audited. The same year, among corporations with assets under $250,000, less than 1% were audited, while 2% of those with assets totaling $250,000-$1,000,000 were audited, and the number jumped to 6% for corporations with assets of between $1,000,000 and $5,000,000. It's also interesting to note that the trend has been to decrease the number of audits among Form 1040 and low-end Schedule C filers, as well as among corporations. Between 1993 and 1995, the only increase in the number of audits was among Schedule C filers with over $100,000 TGR (total gross receipts), and among S Corporations.

IRS audits occur with more frequency in different areas of

the country as well as in different states and cities. For example, in the late 1990's, if you were living in the IRS's western district, which includes Alaska, Hawaii, Idaho, California, Washington, Oregon, and Nevada, your chances of getting audited, if you were filing as an individual, were roughly .92 in 100. However, if you lived in the agency's mid-Atlantic district, which includes Delaware, Maryland, Pennsylvania, Virginia, and New Jersey, your chances dropped to a little over .35 in 100. If you lived in Puerto Rico, or filed your tax returns from elsewhere abroad, your chances of being audited were about 1 in 100. Certain metropolitan areas also tend to generate more audits. For example, in 1996 taxpayers filing individually in San Francisco, Los Angeles, and San Jose California, were at the top of the list, averaging about 1.25 audits per 100, compared to Cincinnati, with less than .4 per 100. Manhattan, on the other hand, generated nearly three times as many audits among partnerships as cities such as San Jose and Philadelphia, with just under 1 audit per 100 returns filed. Los Angeles was at the top of the list among corporations, with over 2 audits per every hundred filed, compared to Atlanta and Brooklyn, both with less than 1 per every 100.

Certain professions are more likely to generate IRS audits, specifically those in which the income is typically derived largely from cash. Examples include the fields of medicine, law, and accounting. In many cases, the IRS will single out a profession, such as attorneys, and make them a target for audits no matter what their past history. Additionally, sports stars, and other celebrities are often targeted by the IRS for not reporting certain types of income such as revenue generated from signing autographs, perks for endorsements, and "free" air fare and hotel accommodations.

Your odds of winning an audit in court are decidedly not in

your favor. Tax Court decisions run about 36% in favor of the government and 4% in favor of the taxpayer, with the remaining 60% being split. In district court, the government wins 79% of the cases, the taxpayer 18%, and 3% are split. In appellate court, 89% are in favor of the government, 10% go to the taxpayer, and a mere 1% of the cases are divided.

Just what is the IRS' take if you are audited and don't come out on the winning side? On average, each audit increases the amount of tax a taxpayer pays by about $5,300. You should keep in mind that this number includes audits of very high-end corporations and the figure will be lower for individuals, sole proprietorships, S corporations, and limited partnerships. Colorado, Texas, and Alaska are the states from which the IRS annually gains the largest yield from audits.

Now, even though the odds of winning an audit are obviously low, these odds reflect the national averages. You can dramatically increase your odds if you're prepared for an audit. If you've kept meticulous records and can document everything about your business, your meeting with the IRS won't compare to a moonlight stroll on Maui, but it will most likely at least be tolerable. Remember that the average IRS auditor has between 30 and 50 cases on his or her desk at any given time—and that your audit is nothing personal. If you've kept good records, your logs are in good shape, and you have good representation, that auditor is not going to make any money off you, and will most likely close your case and move on to the next person. In fact, when the decision comes down in your favor, you'll be able to walk away with your pride intact and a well-earned sense of self-satisfaction.

# Just Who are the IRS?

It's tempting, isn't it, to paint the Internal Revenue Service as a wild-eyed, frothing-at-the-mouth monster, with fangs and claws lashing out for our blood (money). In a way, of course, the IRS is monstrous; you'll recall that the United States Tax Code runs some 6,000 pages, and if that's not a monstrosity I don't know what is. However, it's also important to distinguish between the IRS, the institution, and the people who run the IRS. Of the more than 100,000 people employed by the IRS; most of them are just trying to make a decent living and to provide for their families like you and me. Honestly, most of them are not out to get you.

That said, I must admit that I could fill a book twice this size with IRS horror stories that would have your blood boiling with anger. The good folks at the IRS get frustrated with lame decisions made by upper management especially when egocentric, unqualified people get the promotions, and when the IRS violates the rights of the American taxpayer. Charles D. Rossotti, current Commissioner of the Internal Revenue Service, said, "It's going to take "between five and ten" years to even make the IRS an "acceptable institution." I take that to mean that today, the IRS is an unacceptable institution, particularly in terms of how it treats its taxpayers.

We in the United States of America have a constitution that guarantees us certain "inalienable rights." You'll remember from your high school civics classes that we have the right to "life, liberty, and the pursuit of happiness," the right to assemble peaceably, the right to speak our minds, the right to choose our ways to worship, and so on. Remember, too, those oft-repeated phrases "innocent until proven guilty" and "presumption of innocence?" Both of these refer to what many believe to be a basic tenet of our government, (though some call it a "legal fiction"). The burden of proof is on the accuser, not the accused. That is, the government can't punish us for something until it proves we've done it. We don't have to prove that we haven't. Well, if this idea is slippery in the United States judicial system, it's even more so with the Internal Revenue Service, whose motto actually seems to be "guilty until proven innocent" or "we think you owe us more so show us you don't, sucker." This can be especially frustrating when you consider the ineptness within the agency, which, by the way, loses some two million tax returns each year. Yet they expect us to bear the burden of proof!

Thankfully, this might be changing. At the National Audit Defense Network we have taken this on as one of our major issues: the burden of proof should not be on the taxpayer. We've even found there are many people inside the IRS who agree with us, and with most of the American public. (Note: We're making some headway here. Recent legislation has changed the burden of proof back to the IRS in some rare cases. We'd like to see it reverted completely to the IRS.)

Of course, it's extremely difficult for Internal Revenue Service employees to speak out about injustices that they perceive and witness. These folks are out there. I recently had a conversation with Jennifer Long, a brave IRS agent who participated in the first IRS hearings back in 1997. Jennifer didn't disguise herself when she testified. While all the other agents wore hoods and used voice changers to hide their identities, Long spoke publicly and honestly about some of the problems she perceived at the Internal Revenue Service. She paid a price. Jennifer told me later that IRS managers punished her for her forthrightness and bravery. Her co-workers were told that if they were seen socializing with her, or spending any time with her, they would be jeopardizing their own careers. She told me this truly saddened her because she believed it was her duty to speak out against what she saw as injustices to the taxpayer. Obviously, if the IRS weren't such a clandestine, "Cold War-like" operation, it would earn the respect of the taxpayers, instead of the disdain most of us have for it today. Of course, that might also serve to displace some of the fear we taxpayers have for the IRS, which is one of the most effective arrows they carry in their quiver.

## The Structure of the Internal Revenue Service

The Internal Revenue Service is divided into four operating divisions:

1. Wage and Investment Income
2. Small Business and Self Employed
3. Large and Mid Size Business
4. Tax Exempt and Government Entities

Each of these four operating divisions has both a collection branch and an examination branch charged with collecting the tax owed and enforcing the tax code. Depending on the type of tax return you file, agents from one of these four operating divisions will be assigned to your case should you wind up owing the government money or if your return is selected for audit.

While many of your questions can be answered by your tax preparation professional and other professionals, and even though the

United States Tax Code is now available on-line, there might come a time when you need to contact a real live employee at the Internal Revenue Service. There might also come a time when a real live employee of the Internal Revenue Service needs to contact you. As always, it helps to know with whom you are talking, so make sure you note their name. By law, an employee of the IRS must give you their name and their badge number without you asking for it. Make sure to write down the badge number because without it you will never be able to find out to whom you spoke. Let's just take a look at who might answer the phone, or be standing on your front porch when you answer the door.

Customer Service Representatives who work for the IRS are the folks who will answer the phone when you call the IRS' toll-free number. These are people trained to answer basic questions about everything from tax forms, to where to send your check, to why your refund is taking so long to arrive. Generally, these representatives have two-year college degrees, though not necessarily in a related field. In lieu of education in the field of taxes or finances, IRS taxpayer service representatives are required to attend a 20-day training course, with three extra days for those who will be dealing with questions related to Form 1040A. Obviously it's possible that you're not always going to get an accurate or correct answer to your questions. How could someone learn, let alone read, the 6,000-page United States Tax Code in 20 or 23 days? With that in mind, and with what you already know about the importance of keeping records, always get the first and last name of the IRS representative with whom you speak, as well as his or her badge number for identification. That way, if his or her information turns out to be inaccurate, and that inaccuracy is reflected in your tax return and then comes back to haunt you in an audit, you'll be on far firmer ground when it comes time to defend yourself.

While the taxpayer rep is only required to have a two-year college degree, auditors must have four-year degrees. Again, the field does not matter. Your auditor might have an undergraduate degree in English; which would explain why she insists on correcting the spelling on your forms but might have trouble with numbers. Perhaps he holds a degree ornamental horticultural, which would explain why he poured the bottled water you gave him onto your dying ficus tree. Either way, their starting salary is probably somewhere in the $15,000 range, topping out at under $35,000.

By the time we reach the level of legitimate Internal Revenue agents, we find people with degrees that actually relate to their career. IRS agents must have four-year college degrees, with at least 30 semester units in accounting, although in some cases, experience in the field (an internship, work for a CPA, etc.) can count toward those units. Salaries generally start under $20,000 and max out at about $45,000, which is important to consider when dealing with them. A friend of mine is a college professor, and tells stories of recruiters coming to his campus every spring and interviewing freshly scrubbed, suit-and-tied accounting students, and then aggressively recruiting the best and brightest among them (the "A" and "B" students) to work in their companies. Most of these companies offer very attractive starting salaries, particularly given that these graduates are generally 22-24 years old; $45,000 is not unusual, and jobs that pay more than that are out there. Unfortunately, not everyone who graduates does so with "A" or "B" grades. There are a lot of average "C" grades. Generally where do "average" students often end up? That's right, in the public sector. In the case of average accounting students, many end up going to work for the IRS. This could explain in part the general inconsistencies and seemingly capricious nature of IRS agencies across the country. Ralph Nader's "Tax Reform Research Group" recently created a fictional family and prepared a tax report based on that family's income. Twenty-two identical copies of this report were then sent to 22 different IRS agencies. All 22 were subsequently calculated differently ranging from an $811.96 refund to $52.14 in taxes owed.

# Why Would They Audit Me?

After you have filed your tax return, (and assuming it doesn't get lost at the IRS offices) it will be run through a computerized system that ranks it in terms of the degree to which the computer finds it has audit potential. Once the computer has identified the most likely candidates, the returns are examined by people looking for very specific items. These include:

1. The possibility of unreported income.
2. Reporting below normal income for the profession or business.
3. Deductions out of proportion with income.
4. Losses or below normal yields from investments.
5. Exemptions claimed by non-custodial parents.
6. Forms with errors (i.e., expenses claimed on a wrong form).
7. General inconsistencies.

In addition, certain expenses and deductions will raise eyebrows in certain contexts when they wouldn't in others.  For example, if you're an arborist and spend most of your time pruning unruly southern magnolias and Chinese tallow trees, you're going to have a hard time explaining why you're claiming a deduction for the cost of an Amtrak ticket to Seattle (which isn't to say the deduction can't by definition be legitimate).

I guess it almost goes without saying, if you don't file at all, you're asking for trouble.  Although that usually means you don't make a whole lot of money, it also means you're in a group that really ticks the IRS off.  As a matter of fact, the agency has recently increased the number of employees who track non-filers.

Another reason you could be audited: Someone's mad at you.  The IRS has its hands full and cannot possibly keep up with all the work it needs to as evidenced by lost returns and other major mistakes.  Even though it does have a system for determining a return's "audit worthiness," much of it is still rather arbitrary.  It needs all the help it can get, which sometimes comes in the form of taxpayers reporting other taxpayers.  Have you got a recently-fired employee out there?  Do you have a business partner who thinks he got the shaft when the company dissolved?  Does your former spouse who thinks he's paying more child support than he should?  The IRS loves to hear about it.  If they end up increasing the amount of tax they collect, the informant can be rewarded, generally with 10% of the amount, to a maximum of $100,000.  Interestingly, the number one source of IRS tips is ex-wives; the number two source is former business partners.

# What Happens If I Get Audited?

There are some important things to remember should you ever be audited. The scope of an audit is very clearly, and often very narrowly, defined by an auditor's managers. For example, the auditor might be looking at that rental property you sold three years ago after remodeling the kitchen. Were all your expenses legitimate? Did you have receipts? Do you have the records of the sale? In short, do the numbers add up? In other words, the IRS does not necessarily scrutinize your entire tax return; it will usually ask only for certain specific documents.

Each auditor will be working on between 30 to 50 cases at any given time. They want to bring in more money to the IRS, and in doing so, increase their chances of promotion. If you can demonstrate that its not likely they're going to make much headway in your case, it increases the chances that they'll turn their attention to the other files on their desks. This, of course, is best demonstrated in the form of thorough, accurate, and well-organized records.

# When The Letter Arrives

It's a gorgeous Saturday afternoon in spring and you're out in the front yard mowing the lawn, stopping from time to time to toss the tennis ball to your yellow Labrador retriever. You've been up since dawn, played a round of golf, coached a Little League game, and are looking forward to dinner and a movie later this evening. Life is good. As the mail truck approaches, you kill the engine on your mower and walk to the sidewalk to meet the postman, perhaps to chat for a moment about the beautiful weather. Instead, he shakes his head and smiles ruefully as he hands you your mail. He knows and understands. Turning, you walk back toward your house, shuffling through the mail, looking for something besides junk mail. That's when you spot the ominous looking, legal-size envelope, with an IRS return address. You know and understand. Your heart sinks. This is not a refund nor a letter congratulating your on your wonderfully thorough tax return. This is not notification that IRS has miscalculated and that you have overpaid your last three years' taxes. No, it's notification of an audit.

Your heart beats wildly and your stomach churns but in reality, things aren't that bad. I've intentionally painted a common scenario, but the truth is, if you're smart, and have been paying attention to what I've been saying all along, you don't really have anything to be worried about. You finish the lawn and definitely keep your plans in place for dinner and the movie. You know that on Monday you've got some phone calls to make, and, despite what the letter says, the first one won't be to the Internal Revenue Service.

There are two types of audits: field audits and office audits. Notification for both come from the Examination Division of the IRS. Interestingly, however, the word "audit" has been all but banished from the IRS' vocabulary. Instead, it uses the word "examination." You have, euphemistically, been selected for an "examination" or an "impartial review."

If you receive a letter informing you that you've been selected for an office audit, you will have to send in certain requested records and documentation. You will be notified by mail as to the results of your "examination." Oftentimes, there is no follow-up meeting with an IRS auditor or agent. However, if the IRS finds that your form is incomplete or inaccurate, then you may be called in for a meeting.  On one hand, this kind of audit is to the benefit of the IRS, as it saves time and money, particularly in terms of travel by the auditors themselves.  However, because the IRS also counts heavily on the intimidation factor when auditing taxpayers, the agency often prefers the field audit, in which auditor and taxpayer sit down together with the taxpayer's returns and records and go through them.  Former IRS agents have testified time and time again that they've been sent to training seminars specifically designed to teach them to overcome resistance from taxpayers.  Again, in most cases, only certain parts of the return will be examined, and it's entirely possible that a form you're not certain you filled out "correctly" might not be the subject of the audit and will be ignored by the auditor.

In addition to the office and field audits, there is also the "Automated Collection Service Notice."  This is a computer-generated letter that simply informs you that there's a discrepancy in your return that needs to be cleared up.  More often than not, (of course) the result is that you owe more money.  This might be due to something as simple as an addition or subtraction error or perhaps you inadvertently left a box blank.  Maybe the W-2 and 1099 forms didn't match the figures you've provided.  You'll most likely be asked to respond by phone within ten days and/or provide the missing information.

In any case, like with the audit-notification letters, you don't need to panic.  Nor should you immediately and without professional consultation do what the letter asks you to do.  Instead, as soon as you are notified of any kind of problem whatsoever with your return, you should contact your CPA or tax professional.  Even better, you should contact your audit-defense company.  The National Audit Defense

Network employs only highly qualified accountants, auditors, and tax attorneys trained specifically to deal with these kinds of problems.

There is one kind of letter you might receive that should give you pause, one that should distract you during that dinner and movie. That's the letter from the IRS Criminal Investigation Division (CID). If you receive this letter, or as is more often the case, a visit from an IRS Special Agent who works for CID, it's not because the IRS thinks you've made a mistake but because they believe you're intentionally evading paying the taxes you owe. Your chances of receiving such a letter are slim. The targets of these types of investigations tend to be people who are making money illegally such drug dealers, money launderers, etc. If you get a letter from the CID, know this, you're definitely going to need professional help.

Just remember that no matter what form of audit the Internal Revenue Service is subjecting you to, you must maintain your rights as a citizen and taxpayer, including the right not to be bullied and intimidated.

## The Tax Man (or Woman) Cometh

If and when the time comes to meet your auditor face to face, remember that above all he or she is simply another person doing a job and trying to get along in this crazy world. Sure, she might be trying to impress a boss by nailing an errant taxpayer and hauling in a big take, or he might be incompetent and rude. But, they're still people, and unfortunately you've been drawn into the web of their lives, if only temporarily. Even if they are particularly loathsome, no need to lower yourself to their level.    Being pleasant and firm at the same time will more likely increase the chances that things will go favorably. Here are some things to consider when the time comes to meet your auditor:

1. Show up on time—this should go without saying, as it's only common   courtesy anyway, but it will also reduce the time your auditor spends with your return (she'll be looking it over while waiting for you).

2. Make sure your records are not only in good order, but that they look organized to an objective observer.  Just because they make sense to you doesn't mean they will to someone else. Appearances make a positive or negative difference. If it looks like your documentation is professional, you've gone a long way toward making it so.

3. Never turn over original copies of documents, the IRS has the reputation of "losing" such things.  Make photocopies and give them to your auditor.  It might seem like a hassle at the time, but in the long run it's far better to make three or four copies of each document (for your tax professional, your auditor, etc.) than to risk losing records and information that could turn the audit in your favor.

4. Answer only the questions the auditor asks. You're very much like a witness in a criminal trial, and you'll simplify things tremendously by staying the course. While remaining pleasant, don't get chatty, and never discuss aspects of your return that aren't in question.

5. Ask for documentation and/or citations. If the auditor claims that a deduction, for example, is not allowed, insist on seeing support.

6. For your own documentation, tape-record the audit itself (videotaping is not allowed). This will provide you with an exact record of the discussion that transpired and will be more effective should you go to appeal than your notes of the meeting would be. However, be sure to notify the IRS beforehand that you are going to be taping the audit since they will want to be prepared to tape record it as well.

## Your Rights

Although the Internal Revenue Service's unofficial motto might seem to be that the taxpayer is guilty until proven innocent, it's important to remember that you have certain "inherent and inalienable" rights, at the core of which is the right to be treated fairly and respectfully. Internal Revenue Service Publication 1, Declaration of Taxpayer Rights (available on-line at www.irs.gov/forms) lists specific rights to which you as a taxpayer are entitled. They include:

• Protection of Rights: the right to complete explanation and protection of your rights by the IRS
• Privacy and Confidentiality: the right to keep your information confidential, as well as to be apprised of why and in what manner the information is being used.

- Professional and Courteous Service: the right to seek recourse if you are not treated in a "professional, fair, and courteous manner."
- Representation: the right to be represented professionally, which includes the right to reschedule any meeting at which your representative is absent.
- Payment of Only the Correct Amount of Tax: the right not to pay any more or less than you owe.
- Help With Unresolved Tax Problems: the right to seek help through the National Taxpayer Advocate's Problem Resolution Program (phone 877-777-4778)
- Appeals and Judicial Review: the right to appeal IRS decisions to the courts.
- Relief From Penalties and Interest: the right to have fees waived if you can demonstrate your error was the result of incorrect advice from an IRS employee (always get names and badge ID numbers).

## Your Audit Results and Your Recourse

You will not likely receive the results of your audit at your meeting with your IRS auditor. Generally, he or she will take your information (which is why you provide photocopies in lieu of originals) back to the district office where it will be further scrutinized. Once that process has been completed, you will be notified by mail in the form of a Revenue Agent's Report (RAR). Ordinarily, such as in cases of Schedule A or Schedule C substantiation of records, this will occur within a month or a month and a half.  Included in the RAR will be recommendations for further action and/or an indication of how much more you owe in taxes and when payment is expected.  You now have four basic recourses:

1. You can accept the agency's findings and pay the amount indicated.
2. You can pay the amount indicated but then file for a refund, typically leading to the United States District Court (see below).
3. You can request an appeal in writing, which you have 30 days to do.
4. You can file an "Offer in Compromise."

When you disagree with the IRS' findings, the frustration that will be involved with an appeal will be enormous.Though it will be tempting to want to appeal on principal even a small amount, in the long run it just might not be worth the trouble.  In a perfect world, the IRS would quickly see the folly of its ways and acknowledge that it erred and that you in fact do not owe that additional $94.37.  In reality, it might take months of phone calls and letters, not to mention psychological and emotional energy, to get your case heard, and even then, you're far from guaranteed that it will turn out in your favor.  If you've got that time and energy, then by all means go for it—the government should be challenged on every penny it claims from taxpayers.  Just know what you might be getting into.

Remember that ordinarily as you go through the appeal process, interest will continue to accrue on the amount you owe.  You can, however, stop that interest from accruing by making an advance payment on the deficiency.  This shows good faith on your part, demonstrating to the IRS that you are serious about your appeal.

If you do decide to challenge the IRS' findings, certain information must be included in your letter. First of all, be sure to provide the reference numbers specific to your case; these numbers will be on the RAR (it couldn't hurt to attach to your letter a copy of the RAR itself). Second, indicate clearly the specific findings with which you disagree. Third, explain with factual evidence why the findings are in error. Fourth, provide documentation in the form of references to Tax Code sections, court cases, and/or authoritative literature for your position. See IRS Publication number five on how to prepare for an appeal.

Your case will be heard at your local IRS office by an appeals officer who has been granted certain liberties in the interest of closing the case and, specifically, in the so-called "hazards of litigation." At this meeting, you can represent yourself or choose to be represented professionally, by an attorney, certified public accountant, or other trained tax expert. Though this meeting is still informal, the National Audit Defense Network recommends, as always, that you not represent yourself unless you're intimately familiar with United States tax law. It's just too easy for the agent to take advantage of your naiveté. Depending on the complexity of the case and the appeals office's inventory, you should get the results of this case in 30-90 days.

Although unusual, the Offer in Compromise can be an attractive option. Essentially, this provides a mechanism by which you both acknowledge your liability for the full amount of the audit's findings and at the same time offer to pay less than that. The IRS accepts only a small percentage of the Offers in Compromise that it receives, and those that it rejects become subject to immediate enforced collection action.

# Taking It To the Courts

If you're still dissatisfied with the IRS' findings, you can take your case through the United States judiciary system although the dollar amount involved will be a consideration.  This process will drag the case out even longer and put a much heavier emotional and psychological drain on you.  Keep in mind that the unwritten mode of operation of the court system is not to make sure citizens are treated fairly but to close cases.  This could work to your advantage, as the case might be quickly decided and both parties could be found partially within the letter of the law and partially in error. The IRS knows that going to court can be a huge and oftentimes non-lucrative investment of time and money.  Therefore, depending on the amount of money in question and the legal principle at stake, it's quite possible that IRS attorneys will negotiate an out-of-court settlement. Although it might wind up being a compromise on your part, it will still be more attractive than paying the amount the IRS is demanding. On top of that, it will save you the pain and expense of going to court.

Should you decide to go to court, you have three options: United States Tax Court, U.S. District Court, and U.S. Claims Court. The U.S. Tax Court is a traveling court, of sorts, comprised of 19 judges who hear cases in the larger cities in the country.   The advantage of going through the Tax Court is that your case is heard before you pay the amount in question.  For information on filing with the Tax Court, write to:  400 2nd St. NW, Washington, D.C. 20217 or phone (202) 606-8754 or www.ustaxcourt.gov.

The advantage of the U.S. District Court is that it offers you a jury trial. On the other hand, you must pay your tax bill before your case is heard. See your local phone book under "United States Government-Courts" for your district court office.

All appeals with the U.S. Claims Court are heard in Washington, D.C., by a judge. To determine whether you are a candidate, your case must initially be heard before a fact-finding trial judge in your appropriate geographical district. For information write to: Clerk of the Court of Claims, 1717 Madison Place NW, Washington, D.C. 20005.

# Chapter Sixteen

# National Audit Defense Network's Top 10 List of Taxpayer Mistakes

*"Let knowledge grow from more to more."*
**-Alfred Lord Tennyson,** *In Memoriam*

*"Experience is the name everyone gives to mistakes...Life would be very dull without them."*
**-Oscar Wilde,** *Lady Windermere's Fan*

Everyone makes mistakes. Given the complexity of the Tax Code and the forms on which you must file your return, it's quite easy to make an error. For that reason, I always recommend hiring a tax professional to help you prepare your taxes. On the other hand, you'd be amazed at the mistakes people make that are actually easily avoidable. After going to all the trouble of setting up a home business and maintaining records of income and expenses, to make a thoughtless error—one that could cost you big bucks—is really silly. It's like spending three years restoring a 1956 Thunderbird and then forgetting to wash it on the day of the show.  I think you'll agree with me that even a small degree of common sense, coupled with the healthy skepticism that should attend anyone dealing with the IRS, should keep you from making any of these common mistakes.  However, they're still made, and to an amazingly frequent degree.  The following are the ten most common mistakes we see at the National Audit Defense Network:

**1.  A taxpayer moves without notifying the Internal Revenue Service.**

Obviously, the IRS can find you when and if they need to but sometimes they don't go too far out of the way to do so. If they send you a 30-day notice that you owe tax and you don't respond within this allotted time, the IRS has the right to grab bank accounts and seize assets. I can't tell you how many clients have moved, never received their 30-day notice, and then finally learn that the IRS has tapped their bank accounts when they start bouncing checks.

The IRS makes lots of mistakes—I recently read that some 50% of the deficiency notices it sent out were in error—and you could be sent one even if you don't owe tax. If you don't receive it, you won't know about it, and your bank balance might not be what you think it is.  Note:   Notify the IRS when you move. It's very simple, and it can be costly not to.

**2. A taxpayer does not report an item of income exactly as it appears on the 1099 form or the W-2 received from the employer.**

If the Internal Revenue Service cannot readily identify or

make sense of a figure on your return, they're going to assume that you're in error—remember, you're guilty until proven innocent—and send you a deficiency notice. Other examples include mortgage interest claimed, but which doesn't show up on a matching 1098 form from the mortgage company.

### 3. A taxpayer doesn't file.

This always surprises me. Folks figure that they have a refund coming so they don't need to file. It is true that there's generally no penalty for filing late if you don't owe tax. However, if during an audit the IRS finds that you owe additional tax, there's going to be a 25% late-filing penalty, plus any applicable interest. While it is sometimes possible to have that late-filing fee waived, you must have a pretty darn good reason, and the IRS is generally not very open to waiving it. You have two years and only two years to apply for a refund if the IRS owes you one. If you had a refund due you in 2001 (for your 2000 earnings), you have until April 15th, 2003, to apply for it. Otherwise, it's gone forever. In fact, that two year rule applies across the board in your dealings with the IRS. If they owe you money and you wait more than two years to formally request it, they have absolutely no legal imperative to return it. Here is a case in point: several years ago, an elderly gentleman in California began losing his mental faculties and started writing some very large checks to some very large companies—the phone company, the gas company, and others including the Internal Revenue Service. In total, he wrote tens of thousands of dollars in checks for no reason whatsoever. He sent money to a total of 12 large organizations.

After his death, his daughter, who coincidentally happened to be an accountant, went through his financial affairs and noticed that the checks had been written. Of course, she immediately contacted the companies to whom her father had written the checks, and eleven of the twelve immediately returned the money.   Apparently because it had been more than two years between the since her father wrote the check and she applied to have the money returned, the Internal Revenue Service was the only institution that did not return the money.   Fortunately, the Internal Revenue Service has softened up a bit since then and in cases where it can be proven that an individual was not acting with his complete mental faculties, additional time may be allowed.

### 4. A taxpayer does not file information-only forms.

Another common error is neglecting to file information-only returns, such as 1099s or Partnership returns. Even though you might not have any tax due, the penalties for failure to file can add up very quickly. For example, we've had clients who didn't file form 1065, the United States Partnership Return. The penalty for not filing this form is $50 per month per partner, which can quickly add up to thousands of dollars, even though no tax was initially owed. Again, it is sometimes possible to get these penalties waived, but you're far better off playing by the rules in the first place rather than having to go on the defensive and try to make a case that you're an exception.

### 5. A taxpayer does not keep records long enough.

I've said this elsewhere in this book, but I'll reiterate it here: keep your records!  The general rule is the IRS can audit you for up to three years from the date you file the original return. That means you should keep your records for a minimum of three years. However, remember the IRS truism about being guilty until proven innocent? The burden of proof is on you, the taxpayer. The more documentation you have, the better prepared you'll be to make your case. Don't forget, too, that in certain cases you'll need original documents to demonstrate gains or losses. For example, if you bought a piece of property in 1992 and sell it at a loss in 2004, you're going to need the records from 1992.

I think a good rule of thumb is to hang on to your records five to seven years, or until you just can't find a place for them any longer. If you can stash them out of the way in your garage somewhere, why not?  It certainly couldn't hurt.

### 6.  A taxpayer signs a return without understanding it.

I'll be the first to admit that tax law is neither particularly exciting nor easy to understand, so it makes perfect sense that you'd want to simply sign that form and get it in the mail and out of your life. Remember, though, that your signature makes you responsible for every single item that's been entered on that return. You need to know and understand what you're signing.

You may have heard that the government enacted what they call the "Innocent Spouse Law," a law that basically says the Internal Revenue Service can't penalize one spouse who has no knowledge of the illegal dealings of the other. Well, take that with a grain of salt!  Here is a classic scenario:  a husband and wife file jointly. The wife is a little concerned that the husband isn't filing as, oh, let's say, "cleanly" as he should.  The wife wants no part in it, but she signs anyway to get it over and done with. Big problem! She's responsible for those taxes even if her husband takes off for parts unknown. In fact, if she's available and the IRS can't locate her husband, they'll simply go after her unless she can prove that she qualifies as an "Innocent Spouse".

We recently worked on a case in Tampa where a woman owned a house free and clear and then married an individual who, apparently, had certain questionable tax "situations" in his past, including some rather large liabilities. They were married a couple of years, and then he left the country leaving her high and dry—and with his tax liability. How did the Internal Revenue Service handle it? I'll give you one guess. They took her house, the one she'd owned free and clear before she even met this guy. This was despite the "Innocent Spouse Law."

Our advice in a situation like this is both to understand completely the return that you're filing, and, if you're not sure that your spouse's dealings are on the up-and-up to file separately rather than jointly so that you won't be liable for his or her fines and penalties.

### 7. A taxpayer signs on trust-fund accounts where payroll taxes are held.

It's absolutely critical to keep in mind that everyone who signs on a bank account where payroll taxes are held is jointly and severally responsible for that account. Even if you have no decision-making power in your company, you can be held responsible for that company's tax liability, including fines and penalties. You certainly don't want to get stuck owing thousands of dollars just because you're an honest employee and your boss skipped town to avoid payroll taxes.

### 8. Carelessly depositing cash.

Be very careful depositing cash, as the IRS will naturally assume that any large unexplained cash deposits reflect income, which obviously isn't always the case. We recently had a client who had deposited some cash into his account because he was going to make a purchase for a relative. It was the relative's cash, not his. Of course, the Internal Revenue Service assumed he was depositing personal income. Unfortunately, he hadn't kept records, and had no proof that the deposit did not reflect income, and he ended up in a long and frustrating fight with the government. A gift is not taxable income. If you receive cash as a gift, and you deposit it into an account, be sure to keep records of where it came from. Otherwise, again, you risk having the IRS assume the cash is income.

### 9. A taxpayer utilizes non-viable tax shelters.

Of course you want to decrease your tax liability every way you can, and while one of the best ways to do so is through tax shelters, you need to remember that they need to be shelters that the IRS recognizes as legitimate. We've had many, many clients here at the National Audit Defense Network who came to us after being financially ruined by some of the tax shelters that were offered back in the 1980s. I blame the Internal Revenue Service in part for this because the Tax Code indicated that these shelters were legitimate. After these people had invested in these tax shelters, the IRS went back after the fact and determined that they were not viable after all. Folks had done their financial planning based on how they read the Tax Code, and then the IRS retroactively reinterpreted the language and decided these shelters were no good.  People were wiped out, some losing millions of dollars when they thought they were acting in good faith.  This is yet another reason why you should hire an expert to do, or at least help you, with your taxes.

### 10.  Taxpayers abuse trusts.

Trusts are a valid way to protect your assets.  However, during the last decade or so, a large number of people have been abusing this system.  It's important that you follow the letter and intent of the law.  Back in the '90s, people were setting up trusts and then pointing to questionable language in the Tax Code for justification.  As stated in Chapter 4, if something sounds too good to be true, it probably is.  You need to examine very closely any of those tax-avoidance schemes.  Make sure that someone other than the company representative (who gets a commission when you sign on) can verify that the trust is indeed legitimate in the eyes of the IRS.  Ideally, you will work with a reputable law firm with a long history of working with both trusts and the Internal Revenue Service.

# Chapter Seventeen

# National Audit Defense Network's 25 IRS Audit "Red Flags"

As you know, I *never* advocate that you not take a deduction or credit you are legally entitled to take out of fear of raising an IRS "red flag." The purpose of including this chapter is because I simply want you to be informed of what the IRS looks for when deciding whom to audit. Remember: The KEY to good audit defense is documentation and experienced representation.

## Most Audits Focus on Schedule C

On Schedule C, auditors will be looking for "red flags" such as the following:

1. Gross income over $100,000
2. Nominal income with substantial expenses
3. Cost of goods sold exceeds gross income
4. Cost of goods sold is a high percentage of gross income
5. High auto expense in relation to gross income

6. Substantial depreciation from "listed property" such as computers or automobiles

7. Substantial legal and professional fees regardless of income

8. Substantial insurance expense for a non-medical business

9. Any expense that is large in relation to income or inconsistent to the trade or business. (Actual cases: a janitorial business' expenses for supplies equaled gross income; a service business with cost of goods sold, or a retailer that had large business mileage.)

10. Returns through 1998, when large business mileage and office in the home were mutually exclusive, taking both is a definite flag. Office in the Home is becoming less sensitive due to a change in the tax law.

11. Little or no profit or a loss, especially in a service business.

12. Little income, substantial expenses and a full-time W-2 (indicating little time to make a serious effort at the business).

## Schedule A Issues

On Schedule A, auditors will look for:

13. Excessive medical expenses, especially when there is no apparent ability to pay (wages, interest or dividends indicating savings)

14. Excessive mortgage interest in relation to income

indicating possible unreported income)

15. Charitable contributions in excess of 10% of AGI

16. High miscellaneous deductions, especially high employee business expenses (Form 2106) in relation to W-2 income)

17. Total itemized deductions over 40% of AGI

## Schedule E Flags

On Schedule E, auditors will look for:

18. Rental income less than mortgage interest and taxes (possible related party)

19. High repairs, maintenance or supplies (possible capital expenditures)

20. Depreciation expense on single-family home in excess of $5,000 (home less likely to be a rental, more likely error in computation)

21. High travel cost to property, especially when taxpayer lives nearby

## Form 1040

On Form 1040, auditors will look for:

22. EIC, especially when listing a professional occupation

23. Excessive refund or balance due, especially if due to significant over-or under-withholding

24. Insufficient income to meet claimed deductions (e.g.,

after the medical bills or mortgage or charities or business losses or whatever, how did you live?  Where did you get money for food and clothes?)

# The Biggest Flag and How to Avoid It

25. Any unusual or large transaction.  Include an explanation and copies of documentation with the return and you may avoid an invitation to present your explanation and documents in person.

# Chapter Eighteen

# For Further Information

Although it might seem like you're all alone in your dealings with the IRS—that you're a little David going up against the mighty Goliath—you're not. In fact, a wealth of resources are available to you should you want to continue to learn more about how the IRS functions and how to best prepare yourself for everything from starting a home business, winning an audit, to retirement and estate planning.

## Electronic Sources

One of the great things about the "information age" is how accessible material on tax law is. The entire United States Tax Code, for example, is available online, and although it's very long (6,000 pages) and the language very obtuse and difficult to understand, it's all there for you to read. For full text, go to: http://www.law.cornell.edu/uscode.

Another good place to start is at: http://www.ustreas.gov/tax_regs/index.html.
Here, you'll find links to many helpful sites, including a database prepared and published by the Office of the Law Revision Counsel,

U.S. House of Representatives, that includes the U.S. Tax Code. Another good site is http://www.fourmilab.ch/ustax/ustax.html.

For information on the Internal Revenue Service , check out http://www.irs.gov.

More general web sites, but ones that will provide links to most of the places you want to go, include http://www.irs.gov (the Internal Revenue Service) and http://www.ustreas.gov (Department of the Treasury).

In addition to these sites, the Internet allows you access to chat rooms, bulletin boards and other consumer-based information sites, where you can post questions and engage in give-and-take discussions with other taxpayers. National Audit Defense Network's web site at ***http://www.awayirs.com*** offers you the opportunity to email very specific questions to the former IRS Agents, CPAs and tax attorneys on staff at the National Headquarters.

Armchair Millionaire is an interesting site, offering tax forms and publications, as well as chat rooms and question-and-answer bulletin boards. Check them out at http://www.armchairmillionaire.com.

It should go without saying any information you get from the Internet should be considered carefully for its accuracy and the degree to which it's up-to-date. Remember that literally anybody could be out there offering advice about literally anything. Verify all information you get from the Internet. Don't take a chance on following the bogus advice of someone who has no idea whatsoever what he's talking about.

# Books

If you've taken a look at the financial-planning or tax-help section of your local bookstore lately, you've seen that it's deluged with books on every aspect of taxes and tax law. The shelves are lined with everything from "idiot's guides" to extremely academic and long-winded tomes on the topic. Look closely and you'll see that a lot of them have the same information. They're sort of like a travel guide in that way, or like computer manuals. The best way to choose one is to check the index and table of contents to see if it covers the specific area that most interests you. Then, be sure to read some sample text. You'll find the "readability" factor varies quite a bit. Remember, one of the main reasons you want a tax book is to help you make sense of a tax code that is for the most part incomprehensible. So choose one that does a good job of making the language accessible. Finally, check the publication date. Tax law is constantly changing, and just like with a travel guide, you want one that's as current as possible.

One of the most comprehensive guides to tax law is Jeff A. Schnepper's *How to Pay Zero Taxes* (McGraw Hill). This very readable and exhaustive (over 600 pages) manual is updated annually and includes just about everything you need to know to reduce your tax liability as far as you legally can and just about everything else you need to know about taxes. Chapters include "Benefits for the Elderly," "How to Analyze a Tax Shelter," Investment Planning," and much more, as well as depreciation charts and many other useful graphics.

# Advice of Experts

In addition to these printed and online sources, you should definitely take advantage of the services of a reputable certified public accountant, financial planner, or other tax specialist. Many of the ways this book and others recommend reducing your tax liability can not be done without the assistance of an expert, in many cases a licensed or certified one. Keep in mind that these folks don't work cheap, but there's a reason for that: They're highly trained and can help you save a lot more money in the long run, generally far more than you'll pay them for their services. In addition, the money you spend to have someone prepare your taxes is deductible.

## The National Audit Defense Network

Finally, the National Audit Defense Network offers a wide range of services and information, invaluable to the taxpayer, whether you're an individual, sole proprietor, partner, or CEO of your own corporation. While client services include subscriptions to our newsletters and other publications, as well as access to our information hotlines—all of which provides tax-savings advice that could save you thousands of dollars—the best benefit of your enrollment is that it buys you the best audit defense available. NADN has former IRS agents and attorneys who know the tax code inside and out and who will defend you legally should you find yourself confronted with an IRS audit or a State or local taxing authority.

In addition, NADN is one of the country's leading lobbyists

for tax reform. We pride ourselves on keeping our fingers on the pulse of the nation's taxpayer concerns and doing everything in our power to affect the changes those concerns indicate are necessary. For information about client services, visit our web site at *www.awayirs.com.* You can also get more information by phoning our Las Vegas corporate headquarters at 800-AWAY-IRS (800-292-9477).

# Chapter Nineteen

# Glossary of Terms

**Above-the-line Deductions:**

Deductions made from your gross income to determine your adjusted gross income. Above-the-line deductions include schedule C business expenses, IRAs, alimony, and others.

**AGI (Adjusted Gross Income):**

All the money you earned in a given year, less your business expenses and other above-the-line deductions, not including itemized deductions or exemptions.

**Alternative Minimum Tax:**

An additional tax imposed by the Internal Revenue Code and added to your regular tax if your deductions contain an excessive amount of "tax preference items."

**Annuity:**

Any of several different types of investments defined by your paying for them fixed amounts and then receiving periodic payments for a specifically determined time period or your life, based on standardized actuarial information and tables.

**Audit:**

An examination by the Internal Revenue Service of an individual's or business' tax return(s) for a given calendar year.

**Business Expense:**

The cost of a piece of office equipment, meal on the road, phone call, or other investment in maintaining or increasing the profitability of your business.

**Capital Assets:**

Properties and assets held for investment purposes, including real estate, securities, stocks, as well as for personal purposes, including, for example, your home.

**Capital Gains:**

Income derived from the increase in value of capital assets, including real estate, when that asset is sold.

**Capital Losses:**

Losses incurred from the decrease in value of capital assets, including real estate when that asset is sold or exchanged.

**Capitation:**

"per head" or per person

**Corporation:**

A separate legal entity, even if owned and operated by an individual, that separates the business from its owner(s) for the purposes of profit and liability.

**Credit:**

An allowance that is subtracted directly from the tax liability you owe.

**Deduction:**

A specified amount of money you can reduce from your income, often a business expense, charitable donation, pension contribution, or other legitimate pay-out.

**Depreciation:**

An amount you can deduct for a costly business expense—such as a computer or vehicle—over a period of years, calculated according to its original cost and depreciating values.

**Dividend Income:**

Income earned through any of a variety of investments, when that money is paid directly to you rather than re-invested in the stock, mutual fund, etc.

**Double Taxation:**

A double whammy imposed by the government, for example in the case of an inheritance—assets and/or earnings have been taxed originally, and then they're taxed again to the estate of the decedent before being passed on to heirs.

**Earned Income:**

Wages, salaries, tips, and other employee compensation for professional services and net earnings.

### Education IRA:

An individual retirement account into which money that has been taxed is deposited but whose earnings are not taxed if they're used for the purposes of pursuing higher education, either by the donor or certain beneficiaries.

### Estate Tax:

Tax levied on your assets that are passed on to your heirs after your death.

### Exclusion:

A specified portion of your income that does not have to be included as taxable income. Examples of exclusions: employer-paid insurance policies, workers' compensation, employer-paid educational assistance, and compensatory damage awards for physical injuries.

### Fair Market Value:

Current value of a piece of property or other asset.

### Gift Tax:

Tax levied on high-end (over $2.5 million) estate or other money transfers, which can be as high as 60%.

### Home Office:

A specific portion of your home, whether you rent or buy, which is exclusively reserved for your business, even if the majority of your business actually occurs away from it.

**Individual:**

When used as a noun within the context of business or tax law, an "individual" is a single person not identifying him or herself as a business owner or operator.

**IRA (Individual Retirement Account):**

A retirement account to which you contribute tax-deductible amounts from your paycheck or other earned income. Maximum contribution is $3,000 for an individual, $6,000 for those married and filing jointly.

Note: Except in the case of the Roth IRA (see below), you do not pay taxes on this money when you make the original contributions. Instead, you pay the taxes on these monies when you withdraw the funds upon your retirement.

**Living Trust:**

A trust set up to avoid probate and a mechanism by which your assets may be automatically transferred to your heirs upon your death.

**National Audit Defense Network:**

A national organization established both to provide tax assistance - in the form of audit defense and tax saving strategies - and to lobby for tax reform. Web site: htttp://www.awayirs.com    Phone: 800/AWAY-IRS

**Probate:**

The period during which the legitimacy of a will is being legally established.

**Profit Motive:**

Also known as a "profit objective," this is one of the major criteria the IRS uses to determine the legitimacy of your business. If you can demonstrate that you are making every effort to make a profit, then chances are good that the IRS will deem your enterprise legitimate.

**Profit Sharing Retirement Account:**

Any of a variety of plans by which you can decrease your tax liability by deferring money from your income to specified accounts, often administered by financial-planning companies.

**Refund:**

The amount of money owed to you by the Internal Revenue Service if you have overpaid your total tax from direct salary reductions, quarterly installments, or a combination of the two.

**Roth IRA:**

A recent (1998) addition to the variety of available individual retirement accounts. Money contributed to a Roth IRA is not tax-deductible at the time of the original contribution, but funds are not taxed later, upon retirement, when you make withdrawals from the account.

**Tax Credit:**

An amount that is deducted directly from the amount of tax you owe, generally for an expense such as education or child care.

**Tax Liability:**

A percentage of the amount of your earned income, minus all

deductions which you owe to the Internal Revenue Service, state, and local agencies, for annual taxes.

### Tax Shelter:

Any of a number of different investments for the purpose of reducing your overall tax liability, including individual retirement accounts and real estate investments, as well as home businesses and various corporations.

### Trust:

A figurative "place" where assets are kept, oftentimes for a minor.

### S Corporation:

A business structured in such a way that the owner or owners are responsible for taxable income and/or losses but in which their assets are not legally tied to the corporation and therefor would be exempted in the case of bankruptcy or other legal action.

### SEP (Simplified Employee Pension):

Any of several different types of qualified plans by which you and your employees can contribute to funds whose purposes are to provide retirement income.

### Sole-Proprietorship:

A business owned by a single individual, with all profits and liabilities handled on an individual basis.

### Tax Freedom Day:

That day, generally somewhere toward the end of May, after which the money that a taxpayer earns actually goes to himself rather than to the Internal Revenue Service.

### United States Tax Court:

A court of 19 judges who travel around to the country's major cities to hear cases in which individuals or corporations are in dispute with the Internal Revenue Service. Write to: Clerk, United States Tax Court, 400 Second St. NW, Washington, D.C., 20217; or phone (202) 606-8754 or www.ustaxcourt.gov.

### Write-off:

Informal term for "deduction," an expense that reduces your income for tax purposes.

# HOW TO ENROLL AS A CLIENT OF NADN

## TYPE OF CLIENT SERVICES

❏ Individual 1 Year / $797*    ❏ Business 1 Year/$1195
Ask about our 1 year free Enrollment offer

## CORPORATIONS, PARTNERSHIPS & TRUSTS

Business Name:_____

Federal I.D. #:_____

Street Address:_____

City/State/Zip Code:_____

Phone: (    )_____Fax: (    )_____

## INDIVIDUAL ENROLLMENT

Name:_____

Spouse (For Joint Returns):_____

Social Security#:_____

Street Address:_____

City/State/Zip Code:_____

Work Phone: (    )_____Fax: (    )_____

Home Phone: (    )_____

## METHOD OF PAYMENT
### (payable to National Audit Defense Network)

❏ VISA    ❏ MASTERCARD    ❏ DISCOVER    ❏ AMEX    ❏ CHECK

CARD #: _____EXP. DATE:_____

SIGNATURE:_____

CHECK #: _____AMT. $_____CHECK DATE:_____

## HOW TO ORDER THIS BOOK
To receive additional copies of The Guaranteed Tax Savings System,
call toll-free 1-800-AWAY-IRS (292-9477)
or mail your request with $19.95 plus $6.95 S&H
(made payable to NADN) to the address below

## SEND CLIENT APPLICATION AND/OR BOOK ORDER TO:

*National Audit Defense Network*, 4340 S. Valley View Blvd, Suite 202, Las
Vegas, NV 89103 or fax a request to (702) 889-8825
or call 1-800-292-9477, in Nevada call (702) 889-8820
*Prices subject to change